RIDING IN THE SECOND CHARIOT

A Guide For Associate Ministers

Revised and Expanded

Rev. K. Edward Copeland, J.D.

PrayerCloset Publishing Company, Inc.
P.O. Box 14171
Rockford, IL 61105

Rev. Copeland can be contacted personally at
New Zion Missionary Baptist Church
604 Salter Avenue
Rockford, IL 61102
(815) 964-3114
pastor@newzionrockford.com

Cover/Graphic Designs by Carlton Bruett
ISBN: 978-0-9673519-1-9

Introduction

It is my prayer that this book will be a practical reference guide that you mark up freely and refer to often. Not every chapter is for everyone. Some chapters are written specifically and unapologetically for male ministers. Other chapters are universal in their application and may be used for training lay leaders. In this revised edition I have expanded the most controversial chapters. I have also added some material in order to address some issues that rarely receive public attention. I pray that this little book answers your questions and produces more clarity than confusion.

I want to thank my wife, Starla, and my children, Jibri, Abeni, and Titus for enduring the late nights of writing and editing with grace. Without their patient support this project would have been drudgery instead of a joy. I serve the best church and work with the best ministry team in the world. My ministry team, Brenda Washington, Kim Thomas, Katina Hayes, Min. Deryk Hayes, Min. Charlie Dates, Min. Titus Starks, Min. Wyland Parks and Min. Rodney Hayes have added years to my life by their willingness to pursue excellence in ministry. New Zion Missionary Baptist Church has made pastoring a pleasure.

I also want to thank my spiritual coach Dr. Harold Davis, my mentor Rev. Hezekiah Brady, Jr., my pastor Rev. Lester Cannon, Sr., my father, Rev. William H. Copeland Jr., and my friends Rev. Michael Randle, Rev. Deveraux Hubbard and Rev. Marvin E. Wiley for encouraging me to write.

K. Edward Copeland
July 2004

Chapter 1

MINISTRY FUNDAMENTALS

fun·da·men·tal(s)
A basic and necessary component of something, especially an underlying rule or principle (often used in the plural); the principal tone in a chord, from which other harmonics are generated

A grasp of the basic concepts, principles and skills is essential for success in every field of endeavor. If you would be an all-star basketball player, you must master the fundamentals of dribbling, passing, shooting the ball, spacing the floor, and playing defense. Spectacular slam-dunks will get you on the ESPN highlights but excelling in the fundamentals will get you a championship ring.

Creativity is hampered when the basics are not mastered. You cannot do calculus if you do not know how to multiply. You cannot write poetry if you do not understand sentence structure. You cannot become a chef if you do not know the difference between boiling and broiling. Regardless of the arena you cannot reach your full potential until you learn the basics. Once the fundamentals are grasped, however, there is no limit to what the Holy Spirit can create through human personality.

There are some basic concepts in Christianity in general and ministry in particular that we must constantly review and revisit if we are to prove ourselves faithful and fruitful servants.

There are certain expectations God has for all Christians regardless of their title, function, position or status. Your preaching license is not some sort of VIP card that allows you to bypass the demands that are placed on the rest of the team. If God places you in His starting lineup, that does not mean you get to skip practice. If anything, it means that you ought to show up early. Starters do not slack off in practice; they lead the drills. Similarly, if you have been ordained by God to minister His word then you must help lead the team by example.

> *Don't let anyone look down on you because you are young, but set an example for the believers in speech, in life, in love, in faith and in purity.*
>
> *1 Timothy 4:12 (TEV)*

The word translated "example" in verse twelve is typos in the Greek. It means pattern, model, type, a visual form to be copied, a pattern of behavior to be emulated. What you do or fail to do leaves a visible impression on the rest of the Body. Somebody will ultimately try to emulate you to the benefit or detriment of the Kingdom's cause. Consequently, you need to be sound in the fundamental issues and concerns of the Christian walk.

Discipleship Vital Signs

I recently went to my doctor because I was having sinus trouble. Before the doctor examined me a registered nurse weighed me, took my temperature, my pulse and my blood pressure. Nothing she did was directly related to the problem that brought me to the office. Wisdom and medical expertise dictated, however, that she check my vital statistics. My doctor knows that regardless of what the perceived problem is, it is always wise to check all of the major systems of the body because they all impact one another. The same principles apply to our spirit man. Certain vital signs need to be checked on a regular basis. If we are out of balance in one or more areas of spiritual discipline, then our entire equilibrium will be thrown off and we will be more susceptible to spiritual malaise, infection and disease.

The following is a checklist that points out some of the disciplines that are necessary for any Christian to practice if they are to grow. This list is not exhaustive but crucial. I think it would be difficult for any Christian to grow in a balance way with either of these missing.

I have a daily quiet time.

Whether you call it quiet time, daily devotion, time alone with the Lord or personal meditation period, the point is that every Christian needs some time alone with the Lord on a daily basis. The Bible says that Jesus was accustomed to getting up early in the morning and going to a solitary place to pray. (Mark 1:35; see also Luke 5:16) Job had a habit of getting up early in the morning to offer his sacrifice. (Job 1:5) Daniel made it his habit to meet with the Lord three times a day even in the face of governmental persecution. (Daniel 6:10)

No soldier would dare go into battle without first checking in with his commanding officer so as to receive his orders and hear the strategy for fighting that particular battle. Every day is a battle for the Christian soldier. Wisdom suggests that we talk to the commander in chief before we leave the barracks. He already knows what is going to take place in a particular day and is well able to prepare us for each contingency if we are willing to take the time to listen.

If you have never developed the habit of spending time alone with God on a daily basis now would be a great time to start. The habit of committing your first and best time to communicating with God is like developing a fitness routine. Over time the return on your investment will far outweigh the effort it takes to discipline yourself to do it.

You can purchase and download many classical devotional books and aids online. Some are free. You can download programs that will help you read through the Bible within the course of a year by consistently devoting fifteen minutes a day. Logos Bible software has devotional aids and custom-designed Bible reading programs built in. Another approach that I have found beneficial is to pray through the Psalms or take a particular psalm like Psalms 119 and meditate on a section per day. You might also try reading through the book of Proverbs concentrating on the chapter that corresponds to the day of the month on which you are reading. Since most traditional hymns are based on scripture, your hymnal is a useful tool to cultivate your devotional life. Several exceptional devotional books have been written that detail the story behind the hymns.

However you decide to do it the point is to spend some time alone with God on a daily basis listening to Him speak through His word, talking to Him through prayer and worshipping Him in a private setting.

Have you spent time alone with God today?

I regularly attend and participate in corporate worship at my home church.

There is a big difference between attending a worship service and participating in one. You do not get credit for just showing up, but if you do not show up you can discredit yourself.

I am constantly surprised at how many ministers feel it unnecessary to participate in corporate worship at their home church when they are not preaching. Corporate worship is essential for every Christian but especially for ministers because when God called you to the preaching ministry he called you to a lifetime of listening to His voice. God speaks to us during our private devotions but He also speaks during corporate worship. It is noteworthy that the first missionaries in the New Testament were identified and commissioned within the context of corporate worship.

> *In the church at Antioch there were prophets and teachers: Barnabas, Simeon called Niger, Lucius of Cyrene, Manaen (who had been brought up with Herod the tetrarch) and Saul. While they were worshiping the Lord and fasting, the Holy Spirit said, "Set apart for me Barnabas and Saul for the work to which I have called them."*
>
> Acts 13:1-2 (NAU)

Notice the scripture says that while "they" were worshipping "the Holy Spirit said, . . ." Something unusual happens when the people of God gather together for the purpose of worship. God speaks, reveals, confirms, convicts and encourages during the corporate worship experience in a way that cannot be matched in any other arena.

You need to be in regular attendance at your home churches' worship experience so that you can keep in step with the Holy Spirit as He speaks to that body. I've known associates who love to "visit" other churches when they know that they are not going to preach. The danger there is two-fold. Sometimes they come home with some strange ideas, doctrines and practices that they have picked up from some other ministry. Additionally, constant absence from the corporate worship at your home church insures that you will be out of step with what the Lord is doing in that house. You don't ever want to be in the position of the elder brother Jesus talks about in Luke 15 who had to ask a servant what was going on in his own house. (Luke 15:25-26)

As we experience God and fellowship with one another in corporate worship the Holy Spirit transforms and conforms us to the image of Christ. In worship we are confronted with the reality of God, the comfort of His awesome love for us and the camaraderie of the saints. Corporate worship helps us tune into reality. Worship is what we were created for; therefore, it is one of those fundamentals that we neglect to our own detriment.

Have you been fully engaged in corporate worship lately?

I regularly attend and participate in a systematic Bible study group.

Every teacher needs to be taught. Every preacher needs to be in a regular systematic Bible study in order to maintain vitality. To be healthy you cannot only study the Bible when you are preparing a sermon or planning a lesson you will teach. Just like a cook needs to eat a preacher needs to be fed also.

One of the reasons the church at its inception was the church at its best is because the first believers took the teaching and application of doctrine seriously. The record according to Acts is that "[T]hey were continually devoting themselves to the apostles' teaching . . ." Acts 2:42 The Greek word translated "devoting" in the NAU is proskartere, to join, adhere to; to be ready; to give attention, be faithful; to spend much time together. As the first Christians spent time together paying attention to the apostles' doctrine, fellowshipping, worshipping, and praying they developed a oneness that can only come through sharing the same convictions.

Systematic Bible study will give you a more comprehensive grasp of scripture. Left to your own proclivities you will drift toward studying the topics, biblical characters and sections of scripture that taste good to you. When I was a child I loved to eat Captain Crunch cereal for breakfast. When I would eat breakfast by myself, which was rare, I would automatically grab the Captain. The overwhelming majority of the time, however, we would eat as a family and my mother would fix oatmeal or grits or bacon and eggs. I wanted Captain Crunch but I am grateful into tooth decay and malnutrition. Spiritually speaking, when we only study by ourselves we run the risk of truth decay and spiritual indigestion.

By participating in a Bible study group that is investigating the scriptures methodically, you force yourself to examine scriptural truths that you might otherwise overlook.

> *All Scripture is God-breathed and is useful for teaching, rebuking, correcting and training in righteousness, so that the man of God may be thoroughly equipped for every good work.*
>
> 2 TIMOTHY 3:16-17 (NIV)

Since all scripture is God-breathed and useful, it is to your advantage to have a fundamental grasp on all of it lest you find yourself inadequately equipped to handle the challenges of ministry.

Participating in group Bible study offers the additional benefits of teaching you to navigate small group dynamics and to discern what builds or hampers community. Whether you desire to pastor or not, you would do well to appreciate what it takes to develop a strong Bible study group. Your participation will not only sharpen your biblical acumen but also your people skills.

Have you been consistent in your participation in Bible study?

I daily seek opportunities to share my faith and take the initiative to share when the opportunity presents itself.

Our mission is fishing. The Great Commission is not an option for believers. It is a mandate that cannot be overlooked without suffering the consequences. One of the consequences of not engaging in personal evangelism is that we miss out on the joy of fulfilling our purpose and pleasing our Master. Spiritual balance does not only depend on upreach (worship, prayer) and inreach (discipleship, fellowship, ministry) but on outreach (missions/evangelism).

Preaching from the pulpit is no substitute for personal evangelism. If fishing is truly your mission then you will have to learn how to fish out on the ponds, lakes and rivers and not just in the aquarium.

When someone comes to Christ because of our Sunday morning sanctuary orations, it is analogous to a fish jumping in the boat. The overwhelming majority of fish are not going to jump in the boat voluntarily. They have to be hooked and in order to hook them you have to be willing to go where they are.

The discipline of developing a soul winner's mentality links us up with power that is not accessible otherwise. God does not waste power. He empowers us to do what He wants done. Consequently, there is no need for Him to empower us when we show no interest in doing the primary thing He wants done and that is to be ministers of reconciliation. (2 Corinthians 5:18, 20) The Holy Spirit empowers us to be witnesses. (Acts 1:8) When we refuse or neglect to witness, the untapped power of the Holy Spirit lays dormant in our lives.

Witnessing brings a dimension of joy to our life that is unapproachable by any other means. Nothing can compare to being used by God to bring another person into the kingdom. The only thing that I can think of that comes close is witnessing the physical birth or your biological child.

If you have not been trained in personal evangelism you can begin by learning how to share a one-minute testimony. Your testimony is an indispensable witnessing tool because no one can argue with you about the difference Christ has made in your life. In order to share your testimony in one minute you have to learn how to focus on the essentials. If you were converted at an early age your testimony can be divided into two phases; 1) how you came to know Christ and 2) what difference knowing Christ has made in your life. If you were converted later in life you can use a three-point outline for testimony:

1. Before I met Christ my life was like . . .

2. Here's how I met Christ . . .

3. The difference Christ has made in my life . . .

There are scores of excellent witnessing tools and evangelism training programs on the market right now. You should be familiar with at least three or four different approaches in addition to your personal testimony so that you do not get locked into a preformatted system that answers questions that aren't being asked at the moment. You do not fish for catfish like you fish for sailfish. While the principle is the same, you need a different type of equipment and approach when fishing in the local pond as opposed to the Pacific Ocean. The same is true for evangelism. Though the Word of God is changeless, and ultimately the only thing that can hook a person's soul, different circumstances and cultures necessitate that we learn a variety of ways to get the gospel hook in.

Have you lead someone to Christ recently?

I am developing and maintaining relationships that foster lifestyle accountability.

The Lone Ranger had Tonto. Batman had Robin. Michael Jordan had Scottie Pippen. Who has your back and keeps you on track? The Bible says:

> *Two are better than one, because they have a good return for their work: If one falls down, his friend can help him up. But pity the man who falls and has no one to help him up! Also, if two lie down together, they will keep warm. But how can one keep warm alone? Though one may be overpowered, two can defend themselves. A cord of three strands is not quickly broken.*
>
> ECCLESIASTES 4:9-12 (NIV)

Accountability is such an important aspect of the discipleship process that the Bible never uses the word saint in the singular. The Greek word translated "saint" is always plural in the New Testament. We are responsible for and to one another. Paul uses the analogy of a body to drive home the point that we are accountable to each other.

> *So in Christ we who are many form one body, and each member belongs to all the others.*
>
> ROMANS 12:5 (NIV)

The Bible also implies that God chooses not to deliver us from some besetting sins until and unless we are willing to be honest about our shortcomings with other brothers and sisters in Christ.

> *Therefore, confess your sins to one another, and pray for one another so that you may be healed.*
>
> JAMES 5:16 (NAU)

Certain habits and patterns of behavior are almost impossible to break outside the godly accountability that a Christian friend or small group can provide. Sins of the flesh (sexual immorality, substance abuse, etc) tend to grow like mold and mildew. Mold and mildew grow best in dark damp places. When you let the sun shine in and open the windows so that fresh air can get in, then mold and mildew are deterred. When you keep your pet sins as secrets they tend to fester and grow out of control. When you bring them into the light of godly accountability and allow the Holy Spirit's fresh wind of conviction to purify you, then Satan is disarmed. Accountability allows you to experience true liberty.

If you have no accountability in your life you are living in an unhealthy situation and setting yourself for a fall you might not be able to recover from. During the printing of the first edition of this book President Clinton was in the thralls of the Monica Lewinsky scandal. As this edition goes to print the former president is touring the country promoting his new book, *My Life*. During a poignant interview with Dan Rather on "60 Minutes" President Clinton was asked why he had his affair. His remorseful answer was "just because I could." Translation: "I had too much freedom and not enough accountability." Without appropriate accountability structures in our lives we are all subject to commit senseless acts "just because" we can.

You should develop several layers of accountability. Every Christian needs a Barnabas, a mature Christian encourager who can show us the ropes. You also need a Silas, a brother in the Lord who has your back. Finally, you need a Timothy, someone you are pouring your life into.

Have you built accountability into the fabric of your lifestyle?

I give my time and money to the church consistently, systematically, sacrificially and cheerfully.

Giving is fundamental to discipleship. While you can give without being a disciple you cannot be a disciple without giving. In fact your level of giving is an accurate barometer of your level of commitment. Jesus said,

> *"For where your treasure is, there your heart will be also. . . No one can serve two masters. Either he will hate the one and love the other, or he will be devoted to the one and despise the other. You cannot serve both God and Money."*
>
> MATTHEW 6:21, 24 (NIV)

We are agents of the Almighty. Ministers cannot afford to be stingy and yet claim to represent a generous God.

Tithing is the basement of kingdom giving. If

hypocritical Pharisees were consistent in their tithing, then surely ministers of the new covenant can give above and beyond ten percent. In fact, the tithing principle involves the first ten percent and an offering. (Malachi 3:8) Our offering should be thoughtfully considered, cheerfully given and proportionate to our blessings.

> *Each man should give what he has decided in his heart to give, not reluctantly or under compulsion, for God loves a cheerful giver.*
>
> 2 CORINTHIANS 9:7 (NIV)

God has left specific instructions on how we are to give.

> *On the first day of every week, each one of you should set aside a sum of money in keeping with his income, saving it up, so that when I come no collections will have to be made.*
>
> 1 CORINTHIANS 16:2 (NIV)

The apostle Paul admonishes us to give consistently ("*every week*") and systematically ("*a sum of money in keeping with his income*"). He also points to the Macedonian church as an example of sacrificial giving.

> *Out of the most severe trial, their overflowing joy and their extreme poverty welled up in rich generosity. For I testify that they gave as much as they were able, and even beyond their ability.*
>
> 2 CORINTHIANS 8:2-3

Jesus had more to say about money than any other subject because He knew that our attitude toward material wealth could choke out the efficacy of the Word in our lives.

> *The one who received the seed that fell among the thorns is the man who hears the word, but the worries of this life and the deceitfulness of wealth choke it, making it unfruitful.*
>
> MATTHEW 13:22 (NIV)

Paul echoed that sentiment when he told Timothy:

> *But people who long to be rich fall into temptation and are trapped by many foolish and harmful desires that plunge them into ruin and destruction. For the love of money is at the root of all kinds of evil. And some people, craving money, have wandered from the faith and pierced themselves with many sorrows.*
>
> 1 TIMOTHY 6:9-10 (NIV)

If you are undisciplined your usage of time or money you are a candidate for an impoverished life regardless of how proficient you are in the other disciplines.

> *A little sleep, a little slumber, a little folding of the hands to rest — and poverty will come on you like a bandit and scarcity like an armed man.*
>
> PROVERBS 24:33-34 (NIV)

Have you committed yourself to being a good steward over God's resources?

The Missing Ingredient

Devotional life, corporate worship, Bible study, witnessing, lifestyle accountability, and disciplined giving are essential disciplines to master if you are to maintain a healthy, balanced Christian walk. The goal of these disciplines is conformity to the image of Christ. By listing them here I am not suggesting that Christ-likeness can be achieved by rote submission to some mystical checklist. In fact the list I have laid out is by no means comprehensive. Nevertheless, these disciplines do provide pathways to direct our hearts and minds to love God with our entire being and to surrender to the Holy Spirit on a moment-by-moment basis.

If Christ-likeness is the goal then prayer is the glue that holds the disciplines together and is a discipline in and of itself. Prayer to the believer is like breathing to an athlete. You can master all of the moves, techniques, and nuances of a particular sport or exercise, but if you do not breathe, you will faint. Prayer or spiritual breathing is fundamental to any type of spiritual exertion. The athlete who can control his breathing while mastering the disciplines of his sport can maximize his physical impact. The saint who can prevail in prayer can maximize his or her spiritual impact.

Though they are neglected by many Christian camps, there are at least three corollary disciplines that pay substantial dividends for each unit of time invested in them. By incorporating these three weapons to your spiritual arsenal you will add zest, clarity and focus to your prayer life.

Fasting

Fasting brings clarity and power to your prayer life especially when seeking God's guidance or tackling spiritual malaise or sinful patterns of behavior.

Journaling

Journaling helps you to recognize trends in your spiritual walk and can help you develop consistency in prayer as you recognize and appreciate through your written witness God's faithfulness in answering your prayers.

Scripture Memorization

Scripture Memorization gives focus and weight to your prayers as it enables you to draw upon the reservoir of God's revealed truth to form your requests and direct the conversation. Without a scriptural base, what we call prayer generally reverts to either a recitation of perfunctory religious clichés or a carnal whining session.

Just Do It

For many the admonitions in this chapter may seem so elementary as to not be worth mentioning. Yet how many times do we find ourselves out of pocket, spiritually speaking, simply because we have failed to focus in on some elementary principle? Remember, most athletic contests are not decided in the end by who is the most athletic or who is the most dynamic. The champion is usually the one who has mastered the fundamentals.

Many athletes who were standouts in college or in high school never reach their full potential because once they get the fat contract and the endorsement deal they stop doing the very things that got them him to that level. Do not stop practicing Christianity just because you have "made it" to the pulpit.

Attorneys in Illinois can violate certain traffic laws if they are on their way to court. Theoretically, a lawyer can disobey the speed limit with impunity on the way to court to defend his client who has a speeding ticket. The ones who have taken an oath to uphold the law have provided for themselves a loophole that allows them to break that same law. Such is not the case in the Kingdom. There are no loopholes that allow us to bypass the demands of discipleship on our way to "argue our case" before the Sunday morning jury.

> *Keep putting into practice all you learned from me and heard from me and saw me doing, and the God peace will be with you.*
>
> PHILIPPIANS 4:9 (NLT)

Action Points *Fundamentally Speaking*

- ❑ What fundamental do I need to work on the most?
- ❑ What is my greatest area of strength?

Chapter 2

Inspiration or Indigestion?

I have not sent these prophets, yet they ran: I have not spoken to them yet they prophesied.

Jeremiah 23:21 (KJV)

The elders used to say, "Some were called, some were sent, some just got up on their own and went."

Every true believer has a spiritual gift. Every spiritual gift is to be used in a ministry. (I Corinthians 12:5) Therefore, every believer is called to a ministry. Not every call to ministry is a call to the preaching ministry. Furthermore, a call to the preaching ministry does not necessarily mean that you will ultimately be called to be a pastor.

> *For the body is not one member, but many...All are not apostles, are they? All are not prophets, are they? All are not teachers, are they?*
>
> I Corinthians 12:14,29 (NAU)

Are you sure that you were called to preach and not to some other ministry? Were those strange dreams and warm feelings deep inside when you received your "call" the result of divine inspiration or simply indigestion? I am not trying to judge God's call on your life. I merely want to raise some questions that you need to answer before you get too far down the road in your ministry.

What do we mean by "called"?

Paul testified that he was called to be an apostle. (Romans 1:1; I Corinthians 1:1) The Greek word translated "called" is an adjective that describes one who has been invited, summoned or appointed. All Christians have responded to God's invitation to salvation. For many people salvation merely means escaping eternal damnation and accepting an invitation to Heaven. An eternal resting place in Heaven is not the only thing He invites us to. He summoned us out of darkness into His marvelous light so that we can be partakers of His divine nature. (I Peter 1:15) He summons us to redemptive suffering and presents Jesus Christ as our example. (I Peter 2:21-24) He calls us according to His purpose so that we can be conformed to the image of our Lord and Redeemer. (Romans 8:28-29)

Every God-called preacher has responded to another call that is difficult to explain to those who have not experienced it. Paul defined it in terms of a divine compulsion or constraint. (I Corinthians 9:16) The Old Testament prophets described in terms of a "burden." (Isaiah 15:1; Jeremiah 23:33; Ezekiel 12:10; Nahum 1:1; Habakkuk 1:1; Zechariah 9:1; Malachi 1:1) Jeremiah said that this divine compulsion or burden was so compelling that he could not stop preaching if he wanted to:

> *And I can't quit! For if I say I'll never again mention the Lord— never more speak in his name— then his word in my heart is like fire that burns in my bones, and I can't hold it in any longer.*
>
> JEREMIAH 20:9 (TLB)

Many preachers talk about having run from their calling. Some speak of dramatic epiphanies while others experience a gradual awakening to God's will for their lives. While God accommodates our individual personalities and temperaments, there are several common themes found among God-called preachers.

One common characteristic among preachers is an irresistible urge to study and expound upon God's word. If you do not love God's word, you have not been called to preach. God's word is the preacher's air, food and water. Without His word the preacher has no purpose in life because His word is all that He has left us with in order to evangelize the lost, to edify the saved, to exhort the discouraged, to confront the disobedient, to comfort the afflicted, to rebuke the wicked, to correct the misguided and to instruct His children in righteousness. Preachers love to study and explain God's word. Ezra's testimony ought to be the testimony of every preacher:

> *For Ezra had prepared his heart to seek the law of the LORD, and to do it, and to teach in Israel statutes and judgments.*
>
> EZRA 7:10 (KJV)

Another common thread among preachers is an overwhelming sense of unworthiness at the point of receiving the call. If you think that you have earned the right to stand as God's representative, chances are you do not know much about grace. Paul expressed his gratitude for being chosen:

> *How thankful I am to Christ Jesus our Lord for considering me trustworthy and appointing me to serve him, even though I used to scoff at the name of Christ. I hunted down his people, harming them in every way I could. But God had mercy on me because I did it in ignorance and unbelief. Oh, how kind and gracious the Lord was! He filled me completely with faith and the love of Christ Jesus. This is a true saying, and everyone should believe it: Christ Jesus came into the world to save sinners— and I was the worst of them all. But that is why God had mercy on me, so that Christ Jesus could use me as a prime example of his great patience with even the worst sinners. Then others will realize that they, too, can believe in him and receive eternal life.*
>
> 1 TIMOTHY 1:12-16 (NLT)

God calls preachers in spite of who they are, not because of who they are. If you feel like you did God a favor by accepting the "call" to preach, you should reexamine your calling. God does not need anyone. If He chose you, He chose you as an act of His sovereign grace. Genuine preachers understand that and are appreciative.

A third attribute that is peculiar to preachers is a gut feeling that you were born to preach and that nothing else will satisfy you. Paul said it this way:

> *For just preaching the Gospel isn't any special credit to me— I couldn't keep from preaching it if I wanted to. I would be utterly miserable. Woe unto me if I don't.*
>
> 1 CORINTHIANS 9:16 (TLB)

Preachers love to preach. They also love to be around good preaching. Nothing satisfies a preacher like preaching or hearing good preaching. When you hear good preaching it ought to tickle your "preaching bone" and stimulate you to look at the text again to see what else you can dig out. If you have been called to preach, you feel like you are in your groove when you preach.

That is not to say that you will ever feel that you have mastered preaching or that you will never get nervous when you stand in the pulpit. A fish knows that it is supposed to be in the water even if it has to swim against the current. A bird knows that it was built to fly even when it is flying in stormy weather. Preaching is hard work. Real preachers know that they were designed by God to flourish in this arena despite the accompanying difficulties.

A fourth constant among those who have been called to preach is a godly love for people. A preacher who does not love people is as out of place as a teacher who does not like students or an accountant who does not like to work with figures. Some things come with the job. People and their problems are the stuff that ministry is made of. More importantly the way we relate to the people of God speaks accurately about our love for Christ. In John 21:15-17 Jesus implies that the way we can show our love for Him is be tending and feeding His flock. If you do not love people, it is a sure sign that God has not called you to help watch over them.

WHO "CALLED" YOU?

"You look like a preacher!" That is what my relatives use to say when I was growing up. Whether preachers have a certain "look" is open for debate. One thing is certain, however; well-intentioned church members and overzealous relatives have tried and will continue to try to push people into the preaching ministry.

God is the only one authorized to appoint people to preach His Word. Though God might use different methods to call different individuals, He never violates His own principles. One principle found throughout scripture is that God personally commissions His prophets. Listen to God's exchange with Jeremiah:

> *The LORD gave me a message. He said, "I knew you before I formed you in your mother's womb. Before you were born I set you apart and appointed you as my spokesman to the world." "O Sovereign LORD," I said, "I can't speak for you! I'm too young!" "Don't say that," the LORD replied, "for you must go wherever I send you and say whatever I tell you. And don't be afraid of the people, for I will be with you and take care of you. I, the LORD, have spoken!" Then the LORD touched my mouth*

> *and said, "See, I have put my words in your mouth! Today I appoint you to stand up against nations and kingdoms. You are to uproot some and tear them down, to destroy and overthrow them. You are to build others up and plant them."*
>
> JEREMIAH 1:4-10 (NLT)

One reason God commissions His prophets personally is the prophet must know to whom he is responsible and by whom he is protected. If people "appoint" you as a preacher, then they can "disappoint" you. Whoever called you has to keep you. Make sure you have been called by someone big enough to meet your every need.

WHAT HAVE YOU BEEN "CALLED" TO?

God has called you to prepare yourself. God does not serve half-baked bread. Moses had to spend 40 years in Pharaoh's courts and 40 years tending Jethro's sheep before he was ready. David had to spend his childhood years as a shepherd and then 17 years as a guerrilla fighter before he was ready. Paul had to spend 3 years in Arabia before he was ready. Do not think that you can be called today and ready to take over the world tomorrow. You have been called first and foremost to preparation.

You should take advantage of all of the formal training that is available to you. Most seminaries now have extension sites and many have online courses. Confer with your pastor about the schools in your area. Make sure you check the statement of faith and the accreditation of any prospective school because there are some disreputable ones willing to take your money. Formal seminary training has the advantage of teaching you to discipline your time and your thinking, familiarizing you with systematic theology and acquainting you with the original languages.

Formal theological training is no substitute, however, for the loving nurture and discipleship that occurs through your local church. If you go to seminary with a shaky foundation and loose ties to a church and a pastor, you are likely to come out of seminary an educated fool. If you go in with a solid foundation, however, and look to your church and pastor for spiritual growth issues and the school for sharpening your tools, then you will make the most of the experience.

Whether you have the opportunity to acquire formal training or not, if God has called you He has fundamentally called you into a deeper relationship with Him. The prescription for knowing Him better is easy to understand but hard to apply consistently. The ingredients are:

The Word

You cannot know Him apart from spending time in His Word. His Word reveals His character, His ways, and His will. Listen to His Word on a regular basis. Every preacher ought to listen to or read good sermons on a regular basis. You should have a cache of sermons to listen to in your car, at your workplace and at home. Read through the Bible on a yearly basis. Study the scriptures in order to find answers to life's questions. Learn how to memorize scripture so that you can meditate on it day and night. Apply the scripture you know and He will give you greater insight.

Prayer

It is difficult if not impossible to get to know someone you never talk to. Prayer is the primary means by which we commune with God. It is how our wills are submitted to His will and our requests are presented to His throne. Through prayer we learn how to humble ourselves and rely on God's power to do what human ingenuity cannot do. Jesus Christ said that we ought always pray and not faint. (Luke 18:1) The implication is that if you are fainting (i.e., ready to give up, discouraged) you probably are not praying properly. Prayer is an indispensable part of ministerial preparation. If you do not learn how to pray, you will not last long in this marathon we call ministry.

Fellowship/Accountability

You cannot grow spiritually if you isolate yourself. Joshua had Moses. Elisha had Elijah. David had Jonathan. Daniel had his three friends. Even Jesus Christ kept Peter, James and John close to him. Learning how to fellowship with mature Christians is part of preparing yourself for greater ministry. Proverbs 13:20 says, "He who walks with the wise grows wise, but a companion of fools suffers harm." (NIV) Like Paul, you need a Barnabas, someone to school you. Like David, you need a Jonathan, someone to walk beside you and to strengthen your hand in the Lord. Like Elijah, you need an Elisha, someone with whom you can share your knowledge and wisdom. A preacher who prepares himself by interacting in significant ways with other godly ministers is setting himself up for success. A preacher who wastes time in ungodly conversations is setting himself up for failure.

Tribulation

You do not have to look for trouble. If you are a Christian, trouble will find you. Paul reminded Timothy that, "all who desire to live godly in Christ Jesus will be persecuted." 2 Timothy 3:12 (NAU) Just remember that God uses trials, trouble and tribulation to draw us closer to Him. James says that when our faith is tested by trouble our endurance has a chance to grow. As we persevere under trials, we develop Christian character and a keener awareness of God's ability to provide. You cannot preach effectively to the hearts of people if you yourself have never been through anything. Trouble is a part of God's formula for making preachers.

Waiting

One of the hardest things to do is to wait for God's plan for your life to unfold. Waiting is an essential part of ministerial preparation. You might think you should have been elevated to higher heights in ministry by now. Perhaps you feel your gifts are being overlooked. Take heed to Peter's admonition:

> *You younger men, accept the authority of the elders. And all of you, serve each other in humility, for "God sets himself against the proud, but he shows favor to the humble." So humble yourselves under the mighty power of God, and in his good time he will honor you.*
>
> 1 PETER 5:5-6 (NLT)

The only thing worse than waiting is wishing you had waited. Wait your turn; God is not through with you yet. Let God strengthen your character so that it can bear the weight of your gifts. Do not let your gift crush you because you could not wait until you were mature enough to handle it properly. It is in the waiting that you will get to know Him better which, after all, is the whole point of the matter.

Why were you "called"?

You were not called because of your ability. You were called in spite of your ability and in the light of your disability. Moses could not speak well. Jeremiah was too young. Peter was too impulsive. The truth of the matter is no one is "just right" for ministry. God chooses to use crooked sticks to hit straight licks. He does it so that no one can take the credit but Him. Paul pointed this principle out to the Christians in Corinth:

> *Brothers, think of what you were when you were called. Not many of you were wise by human standards; not many were influential; not many were of noble birth. But God chose the foolish things of the world to shame the wise; God chose the weak things of the world to shame the strong. He chose the lowly things of this world and the despised things— and the things that are not— to nullify the things that are, so that no one may boast before him.*
>
> 1 Corinthians 1:26-29 (NIV)

If you have been called, God chose you so that His strength can be manifested in your weakness. Listen to Paul again:

> *I am going to boast only about my weaknesses,. . . I was given a thorn in my flesh, a messenger from Satan to torment me and keep me from getting proud. Three different times I begged the Lord to take it away. Each time he said, "My gracious favor is all you need. My power works best in your weakness." So now I am glad to boast about my weaknesses, so that the power of Christ may work through me. Since I know it is all for Christ's good, I am quite content with my weaknesses and with insults, hardships, persecutions, and calamities. For when I am weak, then I am strong.*
>
> 2 CORINTHIANS 12:5-10 (NLT)

HOW ARE YOU TO FULFILL YOUR "CALLING"?

> *Do your best to present yourself to God as one approved, a workman who does not need to be ashamed and who correctly handles the word of truth.*
>
> 2 TIM 2:15 (NIV)

Ministry is hard work. It requires disciplined preparation and personal tenacity. Persistence and perseverance are indispensable if you would fulfill your calling. Ministry is not for wimps. Paul's final words to Timothy are worth reading every day:

> *Preach the word of God. Be persistent,*

> *whether the time is favorable or not. Patiently correct, rebuke, and encourage your people with good teaching. For a time is coming when people will no longer listen to right teaching. They will follow their own desires and will look for teachers who will tell them whatever they want to hear. They will reject the truth and follow strange myths. But you should keep a clear mind in every situation. Don't be afraid of suffering for the Lord. Work at bringing others to Christ. Complete the ministry God has given you.*
>
> 2 TIMOTHY 4:2-5 (NLT)

Be yourself. There is nothing wrong with looking up to someone, but remember you are a designer original. God has made each person divinely peerless. He works through the idiosyncrasies of our individual personalities. The pastor you serve under is unique also. Do not allow your admiration of a particular preacher or personality cause you to trade in your uniqueness in order to become a cheap "knock off" of the original. Emulate but do not imitate. Be yourself but be your best self. Incorporate your pastor's positive qualities into your own personality. Identify his negative qualities and make sure you do not duplicate them. (Philippians 3:17)

THE MYSTERY OF MINISTRY

The preaching ministry is an enigma. God has called some people that we would not have called and not called some we would have. He has the sovereign right to place and position people as He pleases. He does not do it the way we would. He does not go by who is the smartest, the most charismatic, or the most eloquent. That is why it is foolish to compare yourself to anyone else. God does not put people in high positions because they are better or more valuable than others. He does it as an act of His sovereign will. It is all a matter of grace.

> *No one from the east or the west or from the desert can exalt a man. But it is God who judges: He brings one down, he exalts another.*
>
> PSALMS 75:6-7 (NIV)

> *Young men, in the same way be submissive to those who are older. All of you, clothe yourselves with humility toward one another, because, "God opposes the proud but gives grace to the humble." Humble yourselves, therefore, under God's mighty hand, that he may lift you up in due time.*
>
> 1 PETER 5:5-6 (NIV)

Action Points *Inspirationally speaking*

- ❑ How do you know you were called to the preaching ministry and not some other ministry?
- ❑ What are you doing right now to prepare yourself for greater effectiveness in ministry later?
- ❑ Who is your favorite preacher? Why?

Chapter 3

Basic Home Training

There are certain issues of protocol and etiquette that every minister ought to know. If you grew up in church all of this will sound elementary because it all boils down to respect and courtesy. If you did not grow up in church some of these principles may sound foreign to you. You might be coming into the ministry without the benefit of having a pastor who is willing to take the time to explain the basics to you. Perhaps your pastor assumes that you already know certain unwritten codes of conduct. Ask questions if you are unsure about what is appropriate. Pay close attention to the customs and practices of your particular church culture always recognizing that as you travel you will encounter denominational and regional variations. Nevertheless, if you study and apply the following principles you will gain a reputation for being a respectful minister regardless of where you serve.

PULPIT ETIQUETTE

How am I to conduct myself when visiting another church?

Always wait for an invitation from the minister in charge before you take a seat in the pulpit. If you are visiting another church and have not had the opportunity to speak to the pastor or the minister in charge before service begins, sit in the congregation. Do not assume that your presence is required or even desired in the pulpit. If you are so familiar with the pastor and the church that you have a standing invitation to sit in the pulpit, then try to ease your way into the pulpit without drawing attention to yourself. Never walk into the pulpit while someone is preaching unless there is an emergency. Ideally, you should get to the worship service before it starts so you can introduce yourself or make your presence known to the pastor and receive an assignment (e.g., reading the scripture, praying during altar call).

Always acknowledge the pastor who allows you to preach in his pulpit. Pastors, including your own, do not have to let you preach. The pastor is the one whom God has charged with equipping the saints to do the work of the ministry. (Ephesians 4:12) He must give an account for how he watches over the souls in his flock. (Hebrews 13:17) A pastor is showing a great amount of trust and confidence in you by allowing you to minister the Word to his congregation. Additionally, God and the members of the flock are watching to see how you treat God's undershepherd. You cut your own neck if you do not show him the utmost respect.

Always encourage the pastor who allows you to preach in his pulpit. When you become a pastor, you are automatically added to Satan's Most Wanted List. It is impossible for a non-pastor to imagine the type of pressure that a pastor faces daily. Therefore, whenever you have the opportunity to encourage a pastor, make the most of it. (Galatians 6:6-9) He might be on the verge of giving up. Your public encouragement and private affirmation might make the difference. When I am the guest speaker or workshop leader at another church I always send a thank-you note to the pastor who invited me. Common courtesy and gratitude demand no less. (Hebrews 10:24)

Always do what you have been asked to do. If they ask you to pray during altar call, do not sing five verses of your favorite song and then pray a prayer you should have prayed in your private devotion. Pray for the needs of those at the altar. If they ask you to pray an offertory prayer, do not pray for the sick and shut-in. Ask God to bless the offering. If they ask you to pray a devotional prayer, do not pray to Jerusalem and back. Pray for that particular service. It sounds elementary but you would be surprised at how many associate ministers violate this simple principle.

I have seen some try to whip the crowd into an emotional frenzy when they were asked to read the announcements or the scripture. I have seen others try to give a mini-concert when they were just asked to give brief comments. If God has given you the ability to sing or speak, He will also give you the opportunity to exercise that gift in its proper context. In the meantime just do what you have been asked to do and then be seated.

Always support the preacher. My father always says, "You can tell a good preacher from a jackleg. Good preachers support the preacher while he is preaching. Jacklegs just sit there as if nothing is going on." When someone else is preaching, you should be conspicuous in your support of the Word regardless of your personal opinion of the preacher's ability. Jealousy and Envy should have no place in the clergy corps. God has given us different gifts. None is better than the other from the Kingdom's perspective because all are needed.

Some preachers whom you think do not preach as well as you do might very well reach more people than you do if God deems it so. There are those who are hermeneutically limited, didactically dysfunctional and oratorically challenged but are still used greatly by God. The bottom line is, do not despise another man's gift when he is trying to use it to the glory of God.

In addition, do not get jealous of another man's gift because you think he can move a crowd better than you can. No one can do the preaching God has for you. Besides, the Kingdom has more than enough "crowd pleasers". What we need is more "Body builders". (Ephesians 4:11-16) One way we edify the Body is by encouraging one another. So, do not freeze another preacher out while you are sitting in the pulpit. If you cannot say "amen" at least look "amen". Otherwise, get out of the pulpit because you might be quenching the Spirit with your lackadaisical demeanor.

Always treat the pulpit area with the utmost respect. While the worship service is in progress, you should be concentrating on worship. Nothing is more distracting than seeing ministers talking and joking around with one another in the pulpit or with someone in the audience while someone else is speaking. Equally as distracting is a minister who slouches in his seat or sits with bad posture. The people in the congregation are watching you and taking cues from your countenance, your posture and your side conversations. If you treat the pulpit area with disrespect, they will do the same thing to you.

Always speak audibly and distinctly. Learn how to use microphones properly. You may have a message straight from the portals of glory but if the people cannot hear you or understand what you are saying what difference does it make? Listen carefully to how the microphones are set when you are in an unfamiliar setting. When it is time for you to speak, make sure the microphone is adjusted to the proper height. Speak directly into the microphone, but do not swallow it. Always keep the microphone between you and the direction you are facing while you speak. If you are called upon to read scripture, make sure you practice reading it before you get up, especially if it is an Old Testament passage with unfamiliar names. You do not necessarily have to dramatize the scriptures but you should read them with vitality and expression.

How am I to conduct myself at my home church?

Be attentive to the needs of your pastor and to visiting preachers. Make sure that the preacher has the proper liquids available (i.e., water, juice, hot tea) before he preaches. If a guest is preaching, find out before hand at what temperature he would prefer his water. Some preachers prefer hot water; some prefer room temperature tap water. You should also make sure that the preacher has an ample supply of handkerchiefs available at the podium. Most preachers sweat profusely during and after a sermon so it is important to keep liquids available and to keep the preacher away from drafts during and after the sermon.

You should familiarize yourself with your pastor's post-sermon routine. Many preachers like to put on some type of covering (i.e., cape, coat or towel around the neck) after they preach so that they will not be adversely affected by drafts. Find out from your pastor what he prefers. Even if some other ministry is usually assigned to serve to your pastor after he preaches, make sure you understand the routine. You might travel with your pastor to an outside engagement where you will be responsible for ministering to him alone. If your pastor or a guest minister needs to change out of their wet clothes after service, gently usher them to the pastor's study or another appropriate room as soon as possible. Otherwise, those members who want to shake hands with the preacher might unintentionally keep him in a drafty situation too long.

Be punctual. You know what time your service starts on a weekly basis so there is no excuse for being late. If an emergency occurs that will keep you from being on time, make sure that you call your pastor or the appropriate staff person to let him know what has happened. Remember: if evening service starts at 6:00 p.m. you have to be at the church no later than 5:45 p.m. in order to start on time. You do not get credit because you are on the premises (i.e., running in from the parking lot) at 6:00 p.m. You need to be in place before the anticipated starting time in order to be "on time". If you do not plan to be early, you are planning to be late.

Be attentive to the flow of the service. Do not disrupt the flow of the service by offering unauthorized commentary or adding elements without pastoral permission. I have seen associates try to sneak in a verse of their favorite song because of the excitement of standing in front of a large crowd. I have seen associates stand to do one thing, say "I just have to say this . . .", and then go on to say something completely irrelevant to the moment or beyond their scope of authority to say. Stick to your assignment. Do not disrupt the flow of worship by trying to maximize your "microphone time."

Be a catalyst for worship. Ministers must be the primary and principal worshippers in the congregation. Your participation in the elements of worship can do a lot to set the tone in the congregation. Rarely will you find a fire in the pulpit that does not eventually spread to the pews. If the configuration of the sanctuary and church protocol allow you to sit in the pulpit then remember the congregation is watching your demeanor and your attitude. If you are not going to be a catalyst for worship, you have no business sitting where you can be seen. Learn how to leave your worries, problems and negative emotions out of the sanctuary. When it is time to worship, worship should be the only thing on your mind. If you have had a particularly challenging week and do not feel like worshipping, then have someone to pray with you before you go into service. Once you enter the sanctuary, you owe the Lord your entire being as a living sacrifice in worship. (Romans 12:1)

Be prayerful in your support of the Preacher. Preaching is hard work. It does not get easier just because you become a pastor. Whether your pastor, a guest speaker or another associate is preaching they should have a guaranteed "amen" from you. You should pray for them before and during the sermon. When someone is preaching, you should not be daydreaming or moving around in the pulpit. If you need to leave before the service is over, then leave before the preaching starts. Do not let the devil use you to distract the preacher. Never forget that the battle we are engaged in is a spiritual one. Spiritual warfare requires spiritual weaponry. (II Corinthians 10:4, 5) One of the greatest weapons that God has given us is prayer. Make it your practice to support the preacher with prayer at every worship service you attend. Paul's prayer request to the church at Colosse is a timely prayer request for every preacher:

> *Devote yourselves to prayer, being watchful and thankful. And pray for us, too, that God may open a door for our message, so that we may proclaim the mystery of Christ, for which I am in chains. Pray that I may proclaim it clearly, as I should.*
>
> COLOSSIANS 4:2-4 (NIV)

Capitalize on guest ministers. Occasionally your pastor might bring in a guest to preach. To the extent you can do so without being obtrusive or meddlesome you ought to take advantage of the knowledge, skill and experiences of visiting pastors, preachers and speakers. You can pick up some invaluable nuggets just by being around the right people. Many of the greatest theological truths and practical insights I have learned have not come from a book but from informal conversations as I carried a visiting minister's bags to his car or dropped him off at the hotel. Pick the brains of visiting ministers because they will almost invariably know something that you do not know.

Do not become too familiar. Regardless of how close you become to your pastor or other pastors in your area never make the mistake of so informal that you discount their position in the presence of others. You might spend time with them personally in their offices or on the golf course or in their homes. Perhaps a pastor has allowed you to call him by his first name or nickname. Discretion demands, however, that in public settings or in conversations with parishioners you should address your pastor by his title be it "Reverend", "Pastor", "Bishop", "Elder", etc. Different cultures, denominations and regions of the country have different concepts of respect so you must learn how to adjust accordingly. My point is that you can never go wrong by showing the proper respect for the spiritual leader. Familiarity breeds contempt so honor your pastor even if he is younger than you are or he is your close friend.

Expect but do not demand to be called upon. Whenever you go to church you should be prepared to preach or make comments even if you are not on program. This is true even if you are visiting a church for the first time. If you were a medical doctor attending a service and a medical emergency presented itself you could not excuse yourself by saying "I'm not on duty now. I didn't come prepared to save anyone's life today." As a minister you must always be prepared to serve the Body with your gifts regardless of the context. Keep a few sermon outlines in your Bible and have at least a sermon or two memorized. Be prepared to preach regardless of the setting. (2 Timothy 4:2)

Being prepared does not mean that you should force your way onto the program. Just because you showed up for worship does not mean that it is your turn. Never put pressure, however subtle, on a pastor to let you preach. If God has given you a message he has also prepared the perfect context for you to preach it in.

Focus on the positive in every worship experience. The late Dr. Manual Scott, Sr. was purported to be such a positive individual that he could find something nice to say about Satan himself. On a particular occasion, when a young man had preached and done a miserable job by all objective standards, some preachers came to Dr. Scott thinking that they had finally found a situation in which he could not say anything positive. When asked about his assessment of the young man's presentation Dr. Scott calmly responded, "He certainly picked a great text!"

Do not get in the habit of picking apart other people's sermons for the purpose of destructive criticism. Train yourself to look for the positive in every situation. A buzzard can pass by a meadow of blossoming flowers and see nothing. Buzzards only look for that which is dead and rotten. A bee can fly by the same meadow and see all the resources it needs to make honey. What are you, a buzzard or a bee?

Action Points *Basic Home Training*

- ❑ In my churches' culture which of the principles in this chapter are considered top priority? Which principles do not apply?

- ❑ Which principle do I need to work on the most?

Chapter 4

Text Selection & Sermon Preparation

Preparing a sermon is like giving birth to a child. It takes time. The gestation period varies from sermon to sermon. One sermon may require three weeks while another may require three days. You must schedule your study time to allow each individual sermon to come full term. You cannot short-circuit the process or you will give birth to an underdeveloped sermon.

Ideally, what you preach should be a distillation or at least a derivation of what God has been speaking to you about in your private devotions. That is one of the reasons maintaining a daily devotion is so vital to ministry. If you have not been listening to God on a regular basis when you do not have to prepare to preach, it will be that much harder to hear His voice when you are preparing to preach. Of course, not everything He shows you in your private study time is for public consumption.

Even when you are studying specifically to prepare a sermon you should learn how to distill the information for public proclamation. Cream rises to the top if given enough time. Allow enough time for the sermon to settle in your spirit so that what you present to the public is just the top portion of what you have studied. You cannot tell it all in one sermon. You should be able to elucidate your thesis within the span of 25 to 30 minutes. Anything longer than that is probably a pastoral sermon and should be left to the pastor to preach. As my father always says, "a sermon does not have to be everlasting to have eternal consequences."

Marinate Before You Grill

Preaching that sticks is preaching that has been bathed in prayer and marinated by meditation in the Word. You can ruin a good piece of meat by rushing it to the grill without the proper seasoning. Prayer and meditation operate like a marinade for the meat of your sermon. Like a good marinade, they make the sermon more palatable and easier to digest. Prayer is necessary because there is something supernatural about preaching. If the Holy Spirit does not energize your words, you will just be making a lot of noise.

Meditation allows the Holy Spirit the opportunity to point out how the Word applies to the challenges of every day living. When you pray and meditate sufficiently you do not have to manufacture excitement about the text. The flavor of the text will infiltrate your very being and listeners will want to taste it for themselves because they see how much you enjoy chewing on it. A good piece of meat will make its own gravy, but only if you marinate it right.

Choosing the Appropriate Text

One of the challenges of preaching as an associate is determining the appropriate text to preach. There is no shortage of passages to choose from; the problem is that there are too many passages screaming to be preached! Sometimes your pastor will assign a specific passage for you to preach (e.g., one of the Seven Last Words for a Good Friday service), or the ministry in charge will give you a theme scripture (e.g., a passage from Psalms for the Choir's Annual Day). Ultimately, however, you should devise some sort of systematic approach to choosing a text, so that you do not waste an inordinate amount of time deciding what to study.

On those occasions when you are free to choose the passage, you should consider several things. Is there a specific scripture that has been speaking to you in a profound way during your quiet time? Does that scripture speak to issues that the majority of your listeners can relate to? Is the text appropriate for the season? If the answer to all of these questions is "yes" then you should prayerfully proceed with that scripture. If the answer to either question is "no" then, you should continue seeking direction from God. For example, you may have been blessed in a special way during your quiet time by studying what Paul has to say about marriage in Ephesians 5: 21-33. But if you know that you will be speaking to a crowd primarily made up of single young adults and teenagers you should find another text that is more appropriate. Similarly, Mother's Day is not the appropriate time to preach about Daniel in the lion's den regardless of how "hot" your sermon on that text is.

Is there something that has happened recently on the national, regional or local level that everyone is talking about? If so, search the scriptures to find out what God says about it. Since everyone is talking about it anyway why not direct them to what the Word says about it? Be careful to study the full counsel of God on the subject. Do not be guilty of promoting your own private opinions or viewpoints when preaching about topics that have political or racial overtones.

Preaching a series of sermons through a short book of the Bible or a long passage of scripture is a useful way to avoid wasting time searching for an appropriate text. In a like manner, preaching a series of sermons on a particular topic helps to maximize your study time. Both of these suggestions require strict discipline, but the rewards are tremendous. When you preach through a book you have to deal with topics and ideas that you would normally skip over or avoid. When you preach a series on a particular topic, (e.g., healing, prayer, forgiveness) it gives you a keener insight and a deeper comprehension of that topic than you could otherwise achieve.

Resist the Urge to Whip the Wolves

One mistake that associate ministers and assistant pastors frequently make is they assume pastoral prerogatives in their preaching. Some issues will arise in your congregation that only the pastor is in a position to address. There are some issues that you can address, but they do not need to be addressed from the pulpit. Never use the preaching moment as an opportunity to retaliate or tell a group of people off. There is too much at stake when the people of God gather for worship for you to center your preaching on negative people and negative issues.

Church people can say and do some mean things. Everybody who comes to your church is not saved, sanctified, and filled with the Holy Ghost. Wolves still dress well in sheep's clothing. Sometimes they will express their canine propensities by bristling and barking at you. At other times they may bite and beleaguer the leader whom you love, admire and respect. In either case, you must resist the urge to use precious preaching time to "whip the wolves" in your congregation.

One reason you shouldn't waste emotional energy crafting "wolf-whipping" sermons is there are too many hurting people in the congregation who need a word from the Lord. If you spend your time and energy whipping the wolves, then who will feed the lambs? Another reason to avoid preaching "wolf-whipping" sermons is the fact that you do not know who will show up on a particular Sunday. The wolves you plan to whip may be on vacation the Sunday you preach. Stick with the gospel. Let the Great Shepherd and your undershepherd handle the wolves.

Preach What You Know Not What You Have Heard

The most effective preaching is preaching that is based on personal experience with God. Anyone can preach a nice, hermeneutically accurate sermon on healing. However, if you have been on your deathbed and God raised you up, your preaching will have a different impact. Anyone can say, "The Lord will provide." However, when you have been down to a zero balance with a family to provide for and He makes a way for you, you can say, "He'll make a way" with conviction. I am not saying that you have to have experienced the exact event that you are preaching about. None of us has ever or ever will be crucified like Jesus was and yet we preach about the cross in every sermon. I am saying that in every sermon there ought to be some universal theme or experience that you can relate to personally.

Do not borrow other people's testimonies. Celebrate what God has done in your life. He does something new every day. You can see His hand at work in your life if you look for it. You do not have to exaggerate in order to have an impact. Just tell the truth truthfully and allow the Holy Spirit to do the rest.

There should be an ongoing conversation between God and you. God is speaking all the time. The question is, are you tuned in to His frequency? There are sermons in your backyard, at your dinner table, in the newspaper, in your car, in your child's conversation and in your favorite television commercials. The principles of God's word are at work all around us. The effective minister keeps his eyes and ears open at all times. You do not know when God might drop a golden nugget right in your lap.

While writing this chapter, God spoke to me through my 20-month-old daughter, Abeni. She was following me around on the second floor of our house. I decided to go downstairs, so I turned off all the lights upstairs and proceeded toward the steps. Abeni knows how to climb up and slide down the stairs by herself, so I started down the stairs expecting her to follow me. As I stepped down to the fourth or fifth stair, I glanced behind me to see where Abeni was. A millisecond later, Abeni launched herself off the top stair and into my arms. She could not see me well because the lights were off. She trusted that I knew where she was, that I could see what she was doing and that I would catch her if she jumped. As I caught her and cradled her in my arms, she giggled at the joy of leaping into her father's arms and then proceeded to play as if nothing spectacular had happened. The Lord spoke to me that day and said, "I know where you are, I see what you are doing, and I'll catch you if you jump." I think that will preach. What do you think?

Study Good Preaching and Effective Communication

Preaching is an art and a skill. With diligent study and practice you can become more proficient regardless of where you start out as a minister. Study the preachers that you love to listen to. What do they do that makes you want to listen? How do they make transitions from the text to contemporary living? What makes their illustrations work? How do they keep your attention once they have it?

You should also study communicators and communication from the secular world. What makes some public speakers engaging even though you do not know what they are talking about and other speakers boring even though what they are saying is important? Why is your favorite commercial so effective? The more you study the art of communication the better you can apply your skills to communicate God's truth.

> *The wise in heart will be called understanding, And sweetness of speech increases persuasiveness. The heart of the wise instructs his mouth And adds persuasiveness to his lips.*
>
> Proverbs 16:21,23 (NAU)

In the final analysis it is the Holy Spirit who gives light and substance to our words. Human effort cannot duplicate Holy Spirit power. Nevertheless, when we discipline ourselves to study, meditate, analyze, illustrate, apply and then study some more, we give the Holy Spirit more to work with. A computer and a typewriter can be plugged into the same power source and both can produce a document but the computer can do more than the typewriter. The shortcoming of the typewriter is not a lack of power from the power source. The shortcoming of the typewriter is its lack of capacity. The computer can do more because it has more to work with. The Holy Spirit has more than enough power. The question is, are you plugged in as a typewriter or a computer? You can increase your capacity if you put some effort into it.

> *Do your best to present yourself to God as one approved, a workman who does not need to be ashamed and who correctly handles the word of truth.*
>
> 2 TIMOTHY 2:15 (NIV)

Action Points *Sermonically Speaking*

- ❏ Develop a series of sermons from a familiar chapter of the Bible (i.e., Psalms 23, John 15, Romans 8, Hebrews 11)

- ❏ Present a different sermon outline to your pastor on a weekly basis whether you will be preaching that week or not.

- ❏ Read your daily newspaper and see how many sermon ideas or illustrations you can gather from the headlines and the advertisements.

Chapter 5

MINISTRY 101: WHAT TO DO WHEN IT'S NOT YOUR TURN TO PREACH

Ministry is more than preaching. In fact, unless you have been called to be a full time evangelist, you will spend the overwhelming majority of your time doing things other than preaching. Do not get discouraged if you do not get the opportunity to preach as often as you would like. God knows all about your situation. The One who called you into this ministry will make sure that you have sufficient opportunities to exercise your gift and validate your calling. If you humble yourself under His mighty hand, He will exalt you in due season. He often lets us marinate on the backside of ministry so that our preaching has the proper seasoning. Seasoned preachers have personal experience with God. Personal experience with God comes from allowing Him to work in your life outside of the pulpit.

Obviously, a delicate balance must be struck. You cannot grow in your preaching ministry if you never preach. Preaching is an art as well as a skill. It takes time and practice to develop your full potential as an oral communicator. At the same time, your proficiency in communicating orally is no substitute for Christian character and the empowering presence of the Holy Spirit in your life.

The message and the messenger ought to be in sync. It is hard to sell hair tonic when you are bald. The tonic might be the most effective product on the market but your slick, shiny, smooth head gives no evidence of the power of your product. The Word of God is alive, active and powerful. If it is not noticeably alive, active, and powerful in your life, however, then those who hear you preach have a legitimate reason to question your credibility. While you are not a perfect Christian, you ought to be a growing Christian. You might not grow an Afro, but if this hair tonic is as powerful as you say it is, you ought to have a few sprigs of new growth to show every now and then.

Unless you are pastoring, it is unlikely that you will be able to decide when you will preach. Some pastors have a regular rotation or preaching schedule for their associate ministers. Other pastors give their associates short notice or require them to preach impromptu sermons. If you know that God has directed you to the church you attend, then you need to submit to that pastor's mode and method of making preaching assignments. While you wait your turn to preach from the pulpit, there are tremendous ministry opportunities awaiting you in your church and community. By serving faithfully outside of the pulpit, you will not only develop Christian character, but insight into how to preach to the needs of people effectively from the pulpit.

Here as some ministry skills you can work on that will strengthen your effectiveness as a preacher and a leader.

LEARN HOW TO LEAD THE WORSHIP EXPERIENCE

Every minister needs to learn how to lead a congregation through the elements of a Sunday morning worship experience. Your demeanor and body language can do a lot to set the appropriate tone for worship. You should read the scriptures with passion and conviction. Your pulpit prayers should be earnest, but not theatrical. If you lead the congregation in singing, then stay within the range of your voice and the realm of your giftedness. If singing is not your forte then speak the words and allow the congregation to sing behind you.

Be sensitive to the mood of the congregation and the movement of the Holy Spirit. If the service seems to be "dry" and the congregation disengaged, learn how to encourage the people to worship without berating them. Scolding people or telling them how dead they look rarely motivates them to worship. Instead, point out something about the goodness of God or why He is worthy to be praised. If the worship service is "hot" and everyone is singing or just rejoicing in general, do not try to cut it short just to get through all the elements in the bulletin. Do not try to grandstand or milk it completely dry either.

Keep Christ as the central focus of your worship and allow the Holy Spirit to direct you when to speak and when to remain silent; when to speed up the service and when to slow it down. In general, you should keep your comments to a minimum. Learn how to say what you need to say in as few words as possible. Few things can quench the Spirit like a worship leader who rambles on and on after each element of worship.

Learn How to Teach Sunday School / Weekly Bible Study

Teaching Sunday School or the weekly Bible study on a regular and consistent basis is like making regular deposits into a savings account. An abundance of scriptural knowledge (or money) can be acquired in a relatively short time if you make consistent and systematic deposits. That is why every minister needs to be involved in Sunday School or small group study or weekly Bible study. If you are consistent in your participation, you will teach through the major doctrines of the Bible within a few years. Additionally, the discipline of preparing your lesson on a weekly basis pays off in large dividends when it comes to sermon preparation. The interactions you have with your Bible study class will not only sharpen your insight, but it can help generate illustrations and examples you could never think of on your own.

Learn How to Visit the Sick, Elderly or Shut-in

Hospitals and nursing homes are not cheery places to visit. Nevertheless, sickness and old age are a part of life. Therefore, visiting the sick and infirm must be a part of your ministry. People are usually grateful to receive a visit from one of the ministers from their church. One of the ironies of life is the fact that I have often been encouraged the most by suffering saints who I have gone to visit in their affliction.

When you visit the hospital be sensitive to the patient's predicament. If possible find out from the attending nurse how the patient is doing and if it is a good time to visit before you enter the room. Knock before you enter their room and announce yourself before you draw back the curtain that separates them from other patients in the room. Do not plop down on the bed and start talking. Find out if there is anything they need done that you can do and ask them for their specific prayer request. Pray for their specific request. If the patient is of the opposite sex and you believe in the laying on of hands, make sure that you take a member of the opposite sex with you who can touch the patient appropriately while you pray.

In general, you should keep your hospital visit brief unless the patient asks you to stay or gives clear indication that they want you to stay. The fact that they are in the hospital suggests that they need as much rest as possible. Nursing home visits can be longer and more involved depending on the health of the individual and the policies of the particular nursing home. If you plan to visit someone who is recuperating at home, do not go unannounced. Call ahead of time to find out the best time of day for a short visit. Get-well cards are always appropriate whether you are visiting the hospital or a home.

Learn How to Preach to Children

If your church has a children's church ministry or some sort of children's moment during the morning worship you should actively participate as much as possible. Not every minister has the gift to work with children, but every minister needs to know how to teach and preach on a child's level. The discipline of simplifying your message so that a child can understand it will serve you well during your ministry. In fact, if you cannot communicate the gospel message on a child's level there is a great likelihood that you are not communicating well with most adults.

Simple illustrations, examples and object lessons are the hallmark of great preaching and teaching. Working with children will help you hone your imagination, creativity and communication skills. You will also pick up some fresh insights and illustrations if you watch and listen carefully enough.

During a recent visit to a friend's church, I noticed a little girl skipping down the aisle during the offertory period with a dollar in her hand. She was obviously overjoyed at the opportunity to give. After she put in her dollar she rushed back to her seat and apparently got another dollar because I saw her skipping past the offering plate again moments later. She gave me a living illustration of II Corinthians 9:7, *"Each man should give what he has decided in his heart to give, not reluctantly or under compulsion, for God loves a cheerful giver." (NIV)*

Learn How to Do Street Evangelism and Outreach Ministry

There is no shortage of sinners in your community. Here's a novel idea; instead of idly waiting for your turn to preach from the pulpit why not "go" and make disciples for Christ? Christ told the original disciples that if they followed him he would make them "fishers of men" not preachers of sermons, twiddlers of thumbs or sitters of pews. Before He ascended, He commissioned us to be "witnesses" for Him. Witnesses testify. You will have more opportunities to share your testimony than you will have to preach. Even if you do not have the gift of evangelism, it is your responsibility as a Christian to share the gospel at every available opportunity. As a minister of the gospel you ought to be at least as excited about sharing Christ with lost souls as you are preaching about Christ to the saved ones. If your church does not already have an aggressive outreach ministry, then ask permission to start one and go hit the streets. You will find fishing is more challenging and rewarding in the lake (community) than in the aquarium (church). You will also be surprised at how hungry people are for the gospel.

Learn How to Follow Up On New Members

How many people join your church but never get active and eventually wind up worshipping on Sunday mornings at Bedside Baptist Church, Mt. Pillow AME or Greater Holy Pajamas COGIC (Church of God in Couch)? Since you do not preach every Sunday why not get actively involved in making sure that new members don't fall through the cracks? If your church does not already have a new membership ministry, then why not help to organize one? If your church already has a new membership ministry, then make yourself available to help in whatever capacity you can. You will never advance so far that you cannot benefit from revisiting the basics. Teaching the fundamental doctrines of Christianity to new believers has a way of refreshing your faith.

Make Yourself Available to Speak at Local Schools, Missions and Jails

An alert minister will recognize and seize opportunities to serve in the community. Local schools need mentors and motivational speakers. The local Salvation Army and other mission's organizations are constantly in need of ministers who are willing to serve. County jails and local prisons have chaplains that are overworked and would love to have more volunteers. All of these venues are fertile areas for fruitful ministry.

I have not listed here all of the possibilities for ministry. One book could not contain all of the ministry opportunities that are available in your community. The next time you feel the urge to complain about not preaching on Sunday morning remember the words of our Savior:

> *Do you think the work of harvesting will not begin until the summer ends four months from now? Look around you! Vast fields of human souls are ripening all around us, and are ready now for reaping. The reapers will be paid good wages and will be gathering eternal souls into the granaries of heaven! What joys await the sower and the reaper, both together!*
>
> John 4:35-36 (TLB)

Pursuing the Vision of the House

Make sure that you are doing all you can to promote the mission and vision of the church you attend. Your church's mission in your community involves more than the Sunday morning experience. Consequently, you should have more than enough work to do if you are concentrating on the mission and not on trying to get to the pulpit.

What if your vision for what the church should be doing is different from your pastor's vision? Associate ministers in teaching settings around the country have posed this question to me. The question always raises additional questions in my mind. If you cannot agree with the pastor's vision for the church, then why are you there? If you were a resident member of your church before your present pastor was installed then you had the chance to vote either "yea" or "nay" to extend him the invitation to pastor. If you voted "yea" then you expressed confidence in his ability to lead and you should let him do so unless you can point to some biblical reason to call for his dismissal. If you voted "nay" then you had your opportunity to voice your dissent and the majority of the Body disagreed with you. Now it is time to either join in agreement with the rest of the Body or to find another place where you can grow. If you came to you present church after the present pastor was already there then you have to answer the question why did you join something you did not agree with? Has the vision changed since you joined or did you join without knowing what you were doing?

If the pastor has changed directions in midcourse or, from your perspective, gotten off course of the stated vision, then you have an obligation to seek clarity from him. In no case should you shoot a hole in the boat you are riding in by overtly or covertly sabotaging the vision.

MAKE SURE YOU ARE IN THE RIGHT HOUSE!

One of the most embarrassing moments of my teenaged years was when my sister and I talked my father into going to McDonalds. At the time my father was not one for eating much fast food so as we stood in line he was perusing the menu in a rather deliberate manner. When it came time for us to order my sister and I chirped out our orders and waited for Dad to place his. He was still looking over the menu. After what seemed an eternity I finally asked, "Daddy, what are you looking for? Maybe we can help you find it." He said, "I'm trying to find the Whoffer (he meant Whopper) but I don't see it." My dad was trying to order a Whopper at McDonalds! He was in the wrong house for what he had a taste for. In like manner, it is possible for you to have a taste for a particular type of ministry that your present church is not equipped to offer. McDonalds fries their hamburgers. Burger King flame grills. If you want a flame-grilled hamburger there is no sense in you going to McDonald's and getting mad because they cannot fill your order. Either order off the McDonald's menu or go to Burger King. If your church does not have what you crave then either settle for what is on the menu or ask God to release you. Remember though you can not always have it your way in the Kingdom.

Action Points *Ministry 101*

- ❑ Write down the mission statement, vision statement, or what you perceive to be the primary focus of the church you attend.

- ❑ What part of that vision/mission statement are you currently and actively engaged in?

- ❑ What are your gift and natural abilities? What specialized training do you have? How are you using what you have to promote your churches vision?

Chapter 6

PROTECTING AND PROMOTING YOUR PASTOR

prot·ect
to defend or guard from attack, invasion, loss, annoyance, insult, etc.; cover or shield from injury or danger.

pro·mote
to help or encourage to exist or flourish; further: to aid in organizing.

Heart attacks, ulcers, high blood pressure and other stress related diseases are prevalent among pastors. Pastoring a church is a high stress occupation. According to a survey commissioned by Leadership magazine, the average pastor works more than 55 hours per week. That figure does not include Sundays. Physiologists have estimated that preaching a sermon is like doing eight hours of manual labor and that an intense counseling session can be like running three miles!

Pastors endure a tremendous amount of pressure on a weekly basis. In addition to the emotional stress of ministry, most pastors face the financial strain of not being compensated appropriately. Pastoring is hard work and it can take its toll on body, soul and spirit. Are you up to the challenge of protecting and promoting your pastor?

A Model Armor Bearer

The account of Jonathan and his armor bearer in I Samuel 14:1-15 is an excellent example of protection and promotion. Notice that the armor bearer's name is never mentioned in scripture. All we know about the young man is that he was devoted, daring and detailed.

He was devoted

This man was willing to follow his leader wherever he went.

> *Jonathan said to his young armor-bearer, "Come, let's go over to the outpost of those uncircumcised fellows. Perhaps the LORD will act in our behalf. Nothing can hinder the LORD from saving, whether by many or by few." "Do all that you have in mind," his armor-bearer said. "Go ahead; I am with you heart and soul."*
>
> 1 Sam 14:6-7 (NIV)

Can your pastor count on your willingness to follow him even when he is going into enemy territory? Are you with your pastor "heart and soul" or do you follow at a distance just to avoid conflict? God can work His plan whether He has to work "by many or by few." Your pastor can work more confidently, however, if he knows that he has a devoted armor bearer. Be the one your pastor can rely on because *"[P]utting confidence in an unreliable person is like chewing with a toothache or walking on a broken foot. Proverbs 25:19 (NLT)*

He was daring

God took what could have been a suicide mission and turned it into a great victory because Jonathan had an armor bearer with some backbone. When Jonathan told his armor bearer what he had in mind his armor bearer said "Go ahead; I am with you ..." When he said, "Go ahead", he did not know how many Philistines where hiding in the rocks. He did not know what types of weapons they had. He did not know if he was going to make it back home that day. All he knew was that God had inspired his leader to try something bold that would help the kingdom. Jonathan had no one else around to depend on. Had his armor bearer balked Jonathan probably would not have taken the initiative to challenge the enemy. This armor bearer's adventurous attitude encouraged Jonathan to do what God wanted.

Notice that the armor bearer was not afraid to demonstrate publicly that he was with Jonathan. The text say, *"Jonathan said, 'Come, then; we will cross over toward the men and let them see us.'... So both of them showed themselves to the Philistine outpost." 1 Samuel 14:8-11 (NIV)* When your pastor takes a controversial stand do you support him privately and then disappear when the heat is on? Your physical presence at a business meeting or board meeting might encourage your pastor and discourage his enemies. You would be surprised at what God could do through your pastor if he had some visible support.

He was detailed

> *Jonathan climbed up, using his hands and feet, with his armor-bearer right behind him. The Philistines fell before Jonathan, and his armor-bearer followed and killed behind him. In that first attack, Jonathan and his armor-bearer killed some twenty men in an area of about half an acre.*
>
> 1 SAMUEL 14:13-14 (NIV)

The enemy "fell before Jonathan" but the armor- bearer followed behind him and made sure they would never rise again. Jonathan led the charge but the armor-bearer did the detail work. Jonathan could not spend a lot of time with individual enemy soldiers because as soon as he engaged one another was upon him. Consequently, the armor-bearer protected his back and cleaned up behind him.

Are you a detail-oriented person? Do you leave loose ends dangling that you know your pastor would have tied up if he had had more time? A good armor bearer sees what his pastor sees and sees what he misses. The devil is in the details. If you understand what you pastor is trying to do then handle the detail work he leaves behind so that he can concentrate on what is before him.

THE SERVANT OF MOSES

Another biblical example of protection and promotion is the relationship between Joshua and Moses. The bible clearly states that Joshua, the son of Nun, was Moses' minister. (Exodus 24:13) He served Moses faithfully and exclusively. Though Joshua was a tremendous military strategist and a brave warrior, he will go down in history as Moses' minister. (Joshua 1:1)

Moses did not fight physical battles. He sent Joshua to do the actual fighting while he supervised. (Exodus 17:8-14) In his supervisory role, Moses had two additional assistants (Aaron and Hur) who supported his uplifted arms on either side. This text indicates that associates and assistants can have different roles and functions depending on their abilities. Some are better suited to be in the field while others are better suited to work up close with the pastor.

Servanthood Development

Your development and progress as a leader is dependent upon and will be no greater than your willingness to serve the leader God places you under. Poor servants make poor leaders. Good servants make good leaders. Great servants make great leaders. If you want to be a great servant, learn how to anticipate the needs of your pastor and to protect his pressure points.

Protect His Time and Energy

The average pastor has to juggle no less than five demanding roles: preacher, teacher, administrator, counselor and civic leader. Husband and father are two roles that offer additional challenges. Any one of these roles can be a full-time job. Consequently, time management is essential for a pastor's well being and the well being of his family. As an associate, you have been divinely placed by God to be your pastor's armor-bearer/minister. You must do all that you can to free up his time so he can devote himself to prayer and the ministry of the word. (Acts 6:4)

It takes time to prepare a good sermon. Help your pastor to find big blocks of time within which he can pray and meditate. When it comes to intense mental work like preparing a sermon the larger the block of time you can be left alone the more work you can do. In terms of creative thinking, the only thing you can do with four hours or less is what you have always done. Since you know how difficult it is to prepare a sermon, you should take the initiative to protect his study time.

Your pastor should not have to concern himself with tasks that anyone could do. Your pastor should not have to open up the church building before service and lock it up after service. He should not have to concern himself with cutting the grass or shoveling the snow at the parsonage. You should be sensitive to and aware of the seemingly small concerns that often consume a pastor's time and sap his energy.

Depending upon the size and structure or your church you might be called upon to do anything from janitorial work to high level strategic planning. Your church might have other ministries that are assigned to some of the tasks I have mentioned. Perhaps the deacons or trustees have been commissioned to handle certain matters. Work with whoever is responsible to make sure the work that has been delegated from the pastor's office gets done so that it does not fall back on his shoulders. The task assigned is not my concern here. The motivation behind your service is. Whatever the task you are assigned you should do it to the glory of God. (Colossians 3:23)

Your pastor should not have to deal with every minor problem that comes up in the congregation. Exodus 18 recounts the counsel Jethro gave to his struggling son-in-law, Moses. Moses was sitting from morning until evening settling disputes between individuals. When Jethro saw what he was doing, he advised Moses to select some able, God-fearing, honest, men of integrity to bear the burden of judging the people. Moses in turn was to concentrate on praying to God on behalf of the people (v.19) and teaching the people God's purpose for their lives. (vs. 20) The same principle was employed in the New Testament when the leaders of the newly formed Jerusalem church encountered a crisis involving the time and energy of their spiritual leaders. Seven spirit-filled men were chosen to handle the crisis while the apostles devoted themselves to "prayer and the ministry of the word." (Acts 6:2-4)

Some pastors have been doing everything for so long that they find it hard to let go and accept help. If you have one of those pastors you must be patient as he builds up confidence and trust in you. If your pastor is elderly or has been burnt by associates in the past, you must do all that you do in a spirit of humility lest Satan play on his insecurities or his emotional scars. You must offer help in a way that does not threaten his position nor give the appearance of usurping his authority. It will be hard for him to let go of the activities and concerns that rob him of his time until he knows that you are loyal and have his best interests and the best interests of the church at heart.

Protect His Reputation and Ministry

A good associate must learn how to minister within the context of a congregation but under the authority of a pastor. God has placed you where you are in order to be a blessing, primarily, to your pastor. Your accountability is to the authority God has set up in your life and not the congregation. Consequently, you should guard your pastor's reputation and learn how to handle his critics.

Do not be a garbage receptacle. First Timothy 5:19 says, *"Against an elder receive not an accusation, but before two or three witnesses."* People should not feel comfortable disparaging your pastor, or any other pastor, in your presence. All gossip, rumor, malicious talk, and innuendo should stop with you. Furthermore, you need to help train others in the congregation on the proper way to handle negative comments about your pastor. Whenever someone comes to me with a negative comment or rumor about my pastor or another minister I immediately ask him or her, "Have you talked to him about it?" When they say, "No", which they invariably do, then I say, "I don't want to hear about it unless you are willing to talk to him about it. Let's go talk to him about it right now!" If they refuse to go with me then I let them know that I will tell the pastor what was said and who said it. Once the word gets out that you are not a garbage receptacle you will be surprised at how the garbage stops flowing your way. More importantly, you will help create an atmosphere of open and direct communication in your church.

Do not swallow everything people try to feed you about your pastor. Just because there is smoke does not necessarily mean there is a fire. Even if there is a small fire do not add fuel to it; try to stamp it out. The Bible says, *"Where no wood is, there the fire goeth out; so where there is no talebearer, the strife ceaseth." Proverbs 26:21 (KJV)*

Do not be a pit bull. Church people will try to sic you on your pastor. If your pastor makes an unpopular decision, or flat out makes a mistake, do not let people pump you up to be the one to "get pastor straight." Church people have a way of manipulating associates to get at the pastor. You have to remember where your loyalties are. You are responsible to God, first, and then to the spiritual authority he has placed in your life. It is not your place as an associate to straighten out the pastor.

Do not join in with the sharks. What should you do if your pastor is caught in a public sin or indiscretion? It depends on whether you are spiritual or not. *"Brothers, if someone is caught in a sin, you who are spiritual should restore him gently. But watch yourself, or you also may be tempted."* (Galatians 6:1) A spiritual associate will find a way to bring restoration to the situation in a spirit of gentleness. Whatever you do, do not join in the feeding frenzy that invariably comes when a pastor's sin becomes public knowledge. When some church people see blood instead of looking for a bandage, they reach for a bib. A minister should be careful to have all the facts before publicly denouncing another minister because words are like spent arrows; once released they are hard to retrieve. Furthermore, there is the law of the harvest that comes into play. Just ask Jimmy Swaggart. One day he got on national TV, pointed the finger at Jimmy Baker and called him a "cancer in the body of Christ" for his financial misdealing. Less than a year later Swaggert was exposed as a whoremonger and had to beg for forgiveness on the same TV program. You do not hear much about Swaggert any more.

First Timothy 5:19-20 says that we should not entertain an accusation against a spiritual leader unless two or three reliable witnesses confirm it. If in fact a pastor or fellow minister is involved in an ongoing sin and refuses to repent, then rebuke is in order.(v.20) Even in rebuke, restoration must be the ultimate goal. Whatever you do, do it meekly. The next time it might be you on the receiving end of rebuke and restoration.

Is it Cancer or a Cold?

I have written with the underlying assumption that the ministry you serve in and the pastor you serve under are reasonably healthy spiritually and emotionally. I realize that some who may be reading these words are in dysfunctional situations and perhaps serving under a pastor who has emotional issues that exceed the range of normalcy.

The biblical principles I have articulated in this book work because the word of God is active and powerful. (Hebrews 4:12) If you are in an unhealthy situation, however, you must apply additional scriptures. Some discernment is required to know which principles to apply and at what time or in what sequence. For example, in order to be healthy physically you must eat properly, exercise frequently, get the appropriate amount of rest and maintain good hygiene. If you come down with the flu, however, you would be too weak to exercise so the best thing to do would be to get more rest. Similarly, there are some principles in this book that might not apply to your current reality because of some imbalance in the relationships. For example, you are not being disloyal to your pastor if you refuse to support his cocaine addiction or if you refuse to cover a lie to his wife while he engages in immoral extramarital activity. If you love the man of God then you should not want to see him destroy his life, his marriage, or the ministry. Gentle confrontation and restoration is the order of the day in such situations.

You have no obligation to support a clear violation of scripture. Too much is at stake to allow sin to run rampant in the camp and infect everyone. Some pastors and ministers never get healed from whatever their sin-sickness might be because those close to them will not hold them accountable for their actions and assist them in finding the appropriate help. The appropriate response is neither to ignore the obvious nor to condemn the weak. Loving discipline with a view toward reinstatement and a minimum of public exposure is the Bible way.

Before you lead the charge to castigate your pastor or some other minister, make sure that you have answered some basic questions:

What are the facts?

Assuming that an offense actually occurred, it is imperative to get the facts. The essential facts and not the lurid details are what must be gathered in order to effectively bring about restoration. Avoid giving the devil too much air time by playing up the sensational aspects of another's sin. Make sure you understand the facts even though you might not understand the motivations and intentions.

Is it a cold or cancer?

Was it a momentary slip or an ongoing pattern of behavior? A cold can be treated successfully with home remedies and rest. Cancer requires specialized treatment by experts with specialized equipment. A minister who succumbs to a temptation in a moment of weakness can be dealt with "in-house" with counseling, restorative discipline, restructured accountability and prayer. A minister who has developed a habitual pattern or lifestyle of alcoholism, drug abuse, embezzlement, physical abuse or sexual misconduct should not be treated with home remedies. Misdeeds that are deliberate, calculated and methodical should not be handled passively. Most good church insurance policies have a provision for professional counseling and treatment. Prayerful consideration should be given to how salvage those directly involved without bringing disrepute on the cause of the Kingdom.

Is the sin public knowledge?

In general, sin should be handled within the sphere of its contact. If the indiscretion is only known and connected to a small group of people, then that is the group that needs to be in on the restorative process. In other words, if a married couple gets into a physical altercation within the confines of their home and no one gets hurt and no one knows about it, then it should not become public knowledge. If that same altercation takes place during a crowded church banquet at a hotel downtown then obviously the entire congregation will have to be addressed at some point. Once something goes public then it has to be dealt with tactfully in a public setting lest people be left to fill in the blanks themselves and run with outrageous versions of the story.

How old are the people are involved?

Consenting adults can be dealt with differently than minors. If a minor is involved in the misdemeanor then special care must be taken not only to deal with the facts but also the perceptions. In no case should action be taken that later could be perceived as covering up or glossing over the incident. Churches are sued for millions of dollars every day for negligently supervising minors and those who are in charge of them.

Consensual behavior between adults does not mean that no action should be taken. In certain situations unhealthy ministers hold as much if not more influence over adults than parents have over children. Lives are devastated when the one ordained to guide and protect becomes the predator. By the same token be discerning enough to know that some people deliberately lay traps for preachers just to watch them fall.

Is the pastor or minister defiant or repentant?

The Bible gives clear direction on how to handle Christians who are caught in sin yet remain defiant.

> *If your brother sins, go and show him his fault in private; if he listens to you, you have won your brother. But if he does not listen [to you], take one or two more with you, so that BY THE MOUTH OF TWO OR THREE WITNESSES EVERY FACT MAY BE CONFIRMED. If he refuses to listen to them, tell it to the church; and if he refuses to listen even to the church, let him be to you as a Gentile and a tax collector.*
>
> MATTHEW 18:15-17 (NAU)

If the person is repentant, however, and willing to submit to the churches' discipline, then the Bible says that we should be careful to reinstate him and reaffirm our love:

> *Sufficient for such a one is this punishment which was inflicted by the majority, so that on the contrary you should rather forgive and comfort [him], otherwise such a one might be overwhelmed by excessive sorrow. Wherefore I urge you to reaffirm your love for him.*
>
> 2 CORINTHIANS 2:6-8 (NAU)

Should law enforcement or some other governmental agency be involved?

If the sin in question is the sexual abuse of a minor then it must be reported. In my opinion, even if you live in a state that does not have compulsory reporting laws, the incident should still be reported. To not do so is to risk that the behavior will go underground and continue. If it happens again and the latest victim can show that the church knew of the offender's propensities, then you can basically say good-bye to any tangible assets the church might own because the church as well as the offender will be sued. Similarly if the sin involves physical violence or destructive behavior it should be reported lest someone lose life or limb.

Action Points *Armor bearer*

- ❑ How often do you pray for your pastor?

- ❑ What is the latest gossip you have heard about your pastor? How did you respond when you heard it?

- ❑ When was the last time your pastor had a vacation?

Chapter 7

THE TRAGEDY OF BEING UNCOACHABLE

"Coming out of high school, I had all the ability in the world but I didn't know the game. Dean (Smith) taught me the game, when to apply speed, how to use your quickness, when to use that first step, or how to apply certain skills in certain situations. I gained all that knowledge so that when I got to the pros, it was just a matter of applying the information. A lot of people say Dean Smith held me to under 20 points a game. Dean Smith gave me the knowledge to score 37 points a game and that's something people don't understand.

MICHAEL JORDAN

FROM HIS BOOK "RARE AIR"

There are thousands of playground legends and local basketball heroes who will never reach the NBA. The reason most will not succeed has nothing to do with their athletic ability but rather one tragic fact; they refuse to be coached. An uncoachable spirit manifests itself in chronic tardiness to practice; a refusal to run the drills correctly; and an inability to take instruction. What made Michael Jordan so great is the fact that he was always willing to be coached.

TEAMWORK NOT INDIVIDUAL TALENT WINS CHAMPIONSHIPS

All great coaches were once great team players. It is no surprise that Doc Rivers, Pat Riley, Phil Jackson and Larry Brown have all become great NBA coaches when you consider the fact that each one of them was at one time a great team player. Each of them sat under the tutelage of a great coach and, therefore, knows what it takes to have a successful franchise. They have earned the respect of the athletes that play for them because their players know they have already been where they are trying to get their team to go.

The 2004 Detroit Pistons shocked the world and proved the point again that it is not individual talent, but teamwork that wins championships. Although their opponent, the Los Angeles Lakers, had the two best players in the world today and a starting line-up that included 4 future hall-of-famers, the Detroit Pistons simply played team basketball and almost swept the series. What was striking about their victory was that each one of the Pistons obviously respected and listened to their coach.

The same principles that work in sports teams hold true for ministry teams. If you cannot be coached as an associate, you will never be an effective coach as a pastor.

God has given a gift to each church in the person of a pastor/teacher. The pastor's God-given role and responsibility is to perfect the saints to do the work of the ministry. (Ephesians 4:12) The word translated "perfect" or "equip" comes from a Greek work that literally means to put a thing in its appropriate position, to establish, to set up to arrange, or to render fit. It can mean to instruct fully or perfectly (Luke 6:40), to refit, repair or mend a broken net (Matthew 4:21) or to restore a disjointed limb. In the context of Paul's discussion on unity in Ephesians chapter four, the idea is that the pastor is the one who trains us, instructs us and helps us to find the position on the ministry team that will maximize our gifts. The tragedy is that in spite of this God-given gift many associates refuse to be coached. What are some of the attributes of an uncoachable spirit?

Shows up late for practice or doesn't show up at all

Can your pastor trust you to be **where** you are supposed to be **when** you are supposed to be there? Does your pastor have to look for you when it is time for prayer meeting or Bible study? What type of reputation do you have in your congregation in terms of dependability and timeliness? From the kingdom perspective the game is won or lost in the solitude of the unglamorous tasks of starting the worship service, teaching the youth Bible study class, preaching in Children's Church, and being on time for each.

Unable to follow simple directions/Showtime mentality

Can your pastor trust you to do **what** you are supposed to do in the way you are supposed to do it? Do you see every request to read scripture or pray in public as an opportunity to sneak in a mini-sermon? Can you be trusted to conduct a worship service without offering unauthorized commentary or personal complaints? Can you be trusted to follow the order of worship as outlined by the pastor without grandstanding for the crowd?

The Holy Spirit is not the author of confusion. He is not going to tell your pastor to move the service in one direction and then tell you something completely different. The Holy Spirit confirms things through the Body. The congregation can tell if the Spirit is leading you. Do not use the pulpit to promote your own private agenda and then blame your foolishness on the Holy Spirit. Do not try to do something spectacular in order to draw attention to yourself and then blame it on the Holy Spirit. The Holy Spirit is intelligent. He never draws attention to anyone but Jesus Christ. So, the next time you feel the urge to preach when you have only been asked to read the announcements make sure the spirit that is prompting you is the Holy one. One sure way to get benched is to come in launching three-pointers and "shooting bricks" when you should be passing the ball.

Relies on individual gifts and skill rather than discipline and teamwork

Can you work with other ministers whom you perceive to be less gifted than yourself? Do you rely on your gifts from the Spirit instead of the fruits of the Spirit in order to make an impact in ministry? Christ-likeness is what gives your ministry impact. A character that is being progressively transformed into the image of Christ is the result of steady intake of the Word, consistent prayer, obedience and the accountability and encouragement that comes from the local fellowship. God does not sanction Lone Ranger Christianity. We are part of the Body of Christ.

> *Think about how this keeps your significance from getting blown up into self-importance. For no matter how significant you are, it is*

> *only because of what you are a part of. An enormous eye or a gigantic hand wouldn't be a body, but a monster. What we have is one body with many parts, each its proper size and in its proper place. No part is important on its own.*
>
> I CORINTHIANS 12:18-20 (THE MESSAGE)

Undermines the coaches authority in the presence of teammates

Have you ever said to someone " Pastor says we should do so-and-so but I say we should . . ." Have you ever murmured or complained to someone else about a decision the pastor made instead of speaking to the pastor directly? Have you ever publicly displayed by your body language and countenance that you were upset with the pastor (i.e., pouted)? If you answered "yes" to any of the preceding questions, you might be positioning yourself to get fired by the General Manager (i.e., the Holy Spirit). You cannot get away with rebellion regardless of how subtle without being penalized.

Won't do what is necessary in order to stay in shape

Can you be trusted to work hard in the off-season? How do you spend your time when it is not your turn to preach or teach? Do you have a daily/weekly routine that will help you stay in shape spiritually, emotionally and mentally?

One of the reasons that some professional ballplayers get hurt is that they stop doing the things that got them where they are. Once the multimillion-dollar contract is signed, they stop conditioning themselves. They come by practice on their way somewhere else, run through a few plays and then leave early without hitting the weight room. Champions who have longevity and play the most consecutive games are those who pay attention to conditioning during the off-season. The same is true for spiritual conditioning. Do not slack off on your personal bible study just because you are not scheduled to preach this Sunday.

Listens to the fans instead of the coach

One of the best ways to get into trouble is to ignore your coach and take advice from the crowd. The crowd will goad you into doing something foolish and then "boo" you when you fall on your face. Church members can be fickle. The same ones that try to put you up on a pedestal Monday might try to crucify you on Friday.

Be careful about taking ministry advice from non-ministers. It is easy to sit in the stands and "second guess" the coach but until you actually get down on the playing field, you do not really know what is involved. Many well-intentioned members feel it is their responsibility to offer their input into your development as a minister. Remember, however, that your pastor is the only one authorized by God to watch over your soul and give a report.

> *Obey your spiritual leaders and do what they say. Their work is to watch over your souls, and they know they are accountable to God. Give them reason to do this joyfully and not with sorrow. That would certainly not be for your benefit.*
>
> HEBREWS 13:17 (NLT)

Action Points *Going for the gold*

- ❑ Are you a team player?
- ❑ What do you do that makes the rest of the team better?
- ❑ When was the last time you helped someone else on the team to look good?
- ❑ Are you typically late or typically early to appointments?

Chapter 8

Aaron's Dilemma: What To Do When Your Leader is Away

One of the most potentially frustrating times to be an associate minister is when your pastor is away. It is potentially frustrating because you might feel pressure from those around you to assume authority that does not belong to you. You might also be tempted to try something "new" that you would not try if your pastor were there. You must resist the pressure to usurp authority whether the source of the pressure is the congregation or your own personal ambitions. At the same time you must make sure that you use the delegated authority you do have to keep the churches' ministries moving until the pastor returns.

Pastoral responsibilities do not take a vacation when your pastor goes on sabbatical. The sick must be visited, the bereaved comforted and the distressed counseled. Bible studies must be taught, prayer meeting conducted and sermons preached. There is a natural tendency to slack off when the "boss" is not around. As an associate, you must fight that natural tendency. If anything, you should tighten up when the pastor is away because the rest of the congregation will be taking their cues from you. If you cannot be trusted to handle the business while the pastor is away, not only will he hear about it but you will lose respect in the eyes of the people. Conversely, if you handle yourself properly when he is away, your pastor is more likely to trust you with more authority and more significant assignments.

Our Lord and Savior left us some noteworthy insight on what to do while your leader is away:

> *The coming of the Son of Man can be compared with that of a man who left home to go on a trip. He gave each of his employees instructions about the work they were to do, and he told the gatekeeper to watch for his return. So keep a sharp lookout! For you do not know when the homeowner will return— at evening, midnight, early dawn, or late daybreak. Don't let him find you sleeping when he arrives without warning. What I say to you I say to everyone: Watch for his return!"*
>
> MARK 13:34-37 (NLT)

COMPLETE YOUR ASSIGNMENT

Notice the man in Jesus' parable gave each one of his employees instruction about the work they were to do while he was away. Each employee had a specific job. Similarly, your pastor will more than likely leave instructions on what needs to be done while he is out of town. If your pastor is not the type that usually gives specific instructions then you should take the initiative to quiz him before he leaves. Are there any errands that you can run while he is away? Are there any meetings that you need to attend on his behalf? Does his family have any special needs that you can meet? (E.g., pastor's daughter needs a ride to recital on Thursday because wife will be at work; car needs to be serviced on Saturday) Check the church calendar to find out if there are upcoming events he would like to have emphasized from the pulpit. Once you find out what he needs you to do then make sure you get it done.

DON'T FALL ASLEEP

When your pastor is away on vacation or a business trip, that is not the time for you to take a mini-vacation. Satan knows when your pastor is away and so do all of his workers. An associate must be especially vigilant while the pastor is away because Satan is an opportunist. He will exploit any opportunity to get a foothold in your congregation. Listen to what Jesus said:

> *The kingdom of heaven may be compared to a man who sowed good seed in his field. But while his men were sleeping, his enemy came and sowed tares among the wheat, and went away."*
>
> MATT 13:24-25 (NAU)

If the devil catches you sleeping, he can sow seeds of discord in your congregation that might take years to weed out. He might sow seeds of rebellion through clandestine and unauthorized meetings regarding church business held in the homes of disgruntled members. He might sow seeds of defiance in the choir when they decide not to show up for evening worship because, "Pastor won't be there." He might even try to sow seeds of pride and arrogance in your heart by having members comment that they prefer your preaching and teaching to that of your pastor's. Always be mindful that the enemy will use anyone he can to do his dirty work. As an associate your responsibility is to keep a sharp lookout, pray without ceasing, and call the devil out when you see him.

Several years ago, my pastor had to have back surgery. At that time he had two associates; I was his assistant and we had recently hired another man as children's minister. For weeks prior to his surgery the pastor met with us, instructed us on what needed to be done during his recuperation, and ended each meeting by asking if we had any questions, problems, or concerns.

On the Sunday after his operation, I conducted the worship service while the pastor was in the hospital recuperating. After morning worship, we were scheduled to travel to another city for a special program. I was to preach at that program in my pastor's place. Immediately after the benediction the children's minister pulled me aside and said that he had some urgent concerns he needed to share with me. He told me that he disagreed with the overall direction of the church, that the pastor's teaching philosophy was unbiblical, and that the Lord had sent him there to "get us straight". I recognized that the enemy was using him at that point and responded accordingly:

1. I did not let him distract me from my assignment. I

pointed out that his timing was inappropriate. I was on my way to complete a preaching assignment given to me by the pastor. I did not have time to get involved in a conversation about something that was not my direct responsibility. When he came to my office he sat down as if he was getting comfortable so we could have a long conversation. I remained standing and opened the door so that he would not feel comfortable sitting down.

2. I let the enemy know that I recognized him. Although this associate was my friend at the time, I let him know that he was out of order. I told him that his concerns were illegitimate and his motive evil. He had been given many opportunities to express any concerns or problems he had directly to the pastor before this incident. His timing gave clear indication that his real motive was to sow seeds of discord.
3. I immediately told the pastor about our conversation. Under normal circumstances, I would not have bothered the pastor while he was recuperating. However, this associate was on staff and working directly with our children and youth. The guile and hypocrisy he displayed by waiting until the pastor was sick to say that he had doctrinal problems with the ministry meant that he was a dangerous person.

During the proceeding months this associate did in fact sow seeds of discord in the congregation that took years to weed out. When the pastor got back on his feet, he requested that minister's resignation. He left with a handful of our members to start his own church. Not surprisingly, that venture fizzled out and all but one of the former members were forgiven and restored to our congregation. Without vigilant prayer, the situation could have been a lot worse. Do not fall asleep when your pastor away. The damage that can be done while you are sleep might be irreparable.

What *Not* To Do while Pastor is Away

One of the most explicit examples of what not to do when your leader is away is found in the book of Exodus.

> *Now when the people saw that Moses delayed to come down from the mountain, the people assembled about Aaron and said to him, "Come, make us a god who will go before us; as for this Moses, the man who brought us up from the land of Egypt, we do not know what has become of him." Aaron said to them, "Tear off the gold rings which are in the ears of your wives, your sons, and your daughters, and bring {them} to me." Then all the people tore off the gold rings which were in their ears and brought {them} to Aaron. He took {this} from their hand, and fashioned it with a graving tool and made it into a molten calf;*
>
> Exodus 32:1-4 (NAU)

In Exodus 24:14 Moses had left Aaron and Hur in charge while he went to get instructions from the Lord. Aaron made at least three critical mistakes in this episode:

Aaron listened to the people

Aaron knew the crowd was wrong. Nevertheless, he let them talk him into using his gift to create an idol god. When your pastor is away, do not let the crowd badger you into doing something foolish. If your pastor has not left specific instructions about a particular matter then leave everything as he left it. Do not try to create something new to appease the people. Fill in the gaps but do not change the format.

Aaron let the people run wild

The King James Version of Exodus 32:25 is intriguing:

> *And when Moses saw that the people were naked; (for Aaron had made them naked unto their shame among their enemies:)*

"Naked" in this context means unrestrained, out of control, wild. Aaron let them do what they wanted to do. In fact, he went along with the crowd.

The old adage is "When the cat's away the mice will play." Well, when the pastor is away members will act a plum fool if you let them! To be fair there are some pastors who have trained and equipped the membership so well that everything runs smoothly when he is away. The majority of churches, however, operate like the children of Israel. Do not make Aaron's mistake. If you see that things are getting out of order, nip it in the bud quickly. You know what your pastor stands for and what he would not allow. The membership does too. Sometimes they just want to see how much you will let them get away with.

Aaron would not take responsibility for his actions.

"The calf just popped out of the oven." That was Aaron's story when Moses got back. If you read the entire chapter, you will find that Aaron *told* the people to take off their earrings. He melted all the earrings. He fashioned the idol. He even built an altar for it. When Moses got back, however, he claimed the calf popped out of the oven all by itself.

If you do make a mistake while your pastor is away, own up to it. Do not blame the people for your decisions. Admit your mistake, accept the consequences and move on.

Action Points *Holding it down*

- ❑ What happened the last time your pastor went away for an extended vacation?
- ❑ Do people at your church act differently when the pastor is away?
- ❑ What ministry at your church seems to suffer the most when the pastor is out of town?
- ❑ Where do people go to get answers when your pastor is not available?
- ❑ If your pastor developed a chronic illness what would your first responsibility be?

Chapter 9

CONFIDENTIALITY: OFF THE RECORD, STRICTLY ON THE QT, AND VERY HUSH, HUSH

The Bible says, "he that repeateth a matter separateth very friends."

PROVERBS 17:9 (KJV)

Loose lips sink all kinds of ships: Relationships, Fellowships, Companionships, Friendships, and Memberships.

During the course of ministering in your congregation, you will be exposed to sensitive information about fellow members. People in crisis tend to turn to their minister for help. Furthermore, if you are actively engaged in hands-on ministry you will be able to discern, detect and decipher some information even before it is orally reported to you. While serving in the children's ministry, you might detect from a child's demeanor that something is "wrong" at home. While working with teens, you might discover that this one is experimenting with drugs or that one is engaging in premarital sex. While ministering to young adults, you might find out that someone had an abortion or that someone else is cheating on his or her spouse. However you discover sensitive information be cautious of how you handle it. Remember that you have several obligations as a minister.

Your Prayerful Obligation

> *Admit your faults to one another and pray for each other so that you may be healed. The earnest prayer of a righteous man has great power and wonderful results.*
>
> James 5:16 (TLB)

Your first obligation is to share sensitive information with God before you decide whether to share it with anyone else. Whether you hear it directly from the person involved in crisis or from an indirect source, do not pass it on without first talking to the One who can actually do something about it. God allows us to be privy to personal information about others so that we can intercede for them. Sometimes our intervention is necessary but never before our intercession. Even when intervention is necessary or when private information about someone's crisis becomes public, a minister must never spend more time talking to people about the crisis than he does talking with God.

YOUR PROFESSIONAL OBLIGATION

As a minister, you have a professional obligation to maintain strict confidentiality if someone shares information with you in your capacity as a minister. Even the law recognizes what is called the "clergy-penitent" privilege. In other words, you do not have to divulge in a court of law incriminating information that was shared with you in your capacity as a minister. There are some notable exceptions. If a person is about to commit a crime and tells you about it, the clergy-penitent privilege does not apply. You should contact the appropriate authorities. Child abuse is another area where the privilege does not apply. In other words, if a child lets you know that he or she is being abused, then you have a legal obligation, in most states, to report it. Check with your local children's welfare agency to find out if clergy in your state are mandated by law to report suspected child abuse or neglect. In my opinion, you should report any incidence of abuse involving a child whether you are mandated or not. The stakes are too high and the consequences too grave to sit on information that might save a child's life or at least his or her innocence. Most states have an anonymous toll free number to report suspected abuse or neglect.

Spousal abuse is unfortunately a prevalent occurrence in our society. Though there are no mandatory reporting laws for spousal abuse, as a minister you should know what resources your community has available. The point of this chapter is not that you should keep quiet about everything you hear regarding families in crisis. The point is that you should share such delicate information only with those who can help to rectify the situation. "Spiritual gossip" or discussing other's personal affairs under the guise of sharing prayer requests or expressing concern should be avoided at all costs. Defamation of character lawsuits are becoming more and more prevalent in church circles. Though your church may have good insurance, nothing can damage a ministry like a breach of confidentiality.

As a minister, you should be cautious when people try to give you too much information. Know when you are in over your head and you need to make a referral. Some issues need to be handled by your pastor. Some people have issues that a trained Christian counselor needs to address. Unless you are certified as a counselor, stay out of that arena. As a minister you can offer spiritual guidance and lead people to find answers from the Bible. Anything more intense than that should be referred out. You can easily get bogged down in someone else's emotional swamp if you do not recognize and respect your limitations.

Unless you are a certified counselor you should not term the assistance you give to parishioners as "counseling." A better term might be "spiritual guidance" or "spiritual coaching." When you hold yourself out to be a counselor then certain rules and consequences apply from a legal standpoint. Counselors are sued on a regular basis by disgruntled clients. Make sure that you are clear on what you can offer and what you are willing to discuss.

Your Personal Obligation

> *Dear brothers, if a Christian is overcome by some sin, you who are godly should gently and humbly help him back onto the right path, remembering that next time it might be one of you who is in the wrong. Don't be*

> *misled; remember that you can't ignore God and get away with it: a man will always reap just the kind of crop he sows!*
>
> GALATIANS 6:1,7 (TLB)

In recent years, I have seen several cases where associate ministers leaked out damaging private information about their pastors. Some were even carnal and foolish enough to lead the charge in ousting the pastor. It is apparent that those who engage in such folly have never read Galatians chapter six. If you are spiritual, you have a personal obligation to bring restoration and healing to situations in which a saint has fallen into sin. That applies to saints in the pulpit as well as the pew.

You might be tempted to share your pastor's personal failures or someone else's private affairs with those who cannot help and are not involved. The Bible calls this gossip. Please remember that "what goes around, comes around." Learn the art of empathy. How would you feel if you were in that person's shoes? Would you want others to know all about the situation? You have a personal obligation as a part of the Body of Christ to pray and keep your mouth shut. The only exceptions to this rule are when criminal conduct is involved or there is an imminent threat of physical harm to someone. Even in those cases where you report something to the appropriate authorities, the entire church does not necessarily need to know specifics. God knows. As a church body, we can pray to Him even when we do not know all the details.

A lot of church strife can be squashed if we as ministers learn when to speak and when to be quiet. *"Fire goes out for lack of fuel, and tensions disappear when gossip stops."*

Proverbs 26:20 (TLB) I like the way Mama says it better, "If you can't say something good, then don't say anything at all."

Action Points *Confidentially speaking*

- ❑ Does your church screen its children's workers? Why or why not?
- ❑ Has any one shared some sensitive information with you recently? How did you handle it?
- ❑ What would you do if you found out that one of the men in your congregation was abusing his wife?
- ❑ What would you do if one of the youth confided in you that they had been molested by one of the youth workers?
- ❑ How would you handle a person who confessed to you that they had just committed a crime?

Chapter 10

What Are You Running From?

Satchel Paige once said "Don't look back; something might be gaining on you." That is sound advice for athletes. In a physical race, it is foolish to run forward while you are looking back. In this spiritual race, it pays to keep your focus on what lies ahead of you instead of what has happened in your past. Nevertheless, if you are not making progress in ministry, perhaps you need to look back to make sure you are not holding on to something from your past.

When I was a teenager several friends and I went to a Haunted House one Halloween. For a small fee you could walk through this house and get scared out of our wits. The house was dark inside and filled with mazes, trap doors and rooms with grotesque scenes. Consequently, my friends and I held each other's hands and went single file through the darkness with me in the lead. I was holding on to my friend Alice's hand when we got to an odd looking room that seemed to have nothing in it. As soon as we relaxed our grips a group of "monsters" suddenly jumped out of their hiding places and surrounded us. We all screamed and panicked. Without looking behind me, I grabbed for Alice's hand and tried to make it to the exit as fast as I could. Alice was not budging and I did not know why. Finally, I looked behind me only to discover that I had grabbed one of the monsters by the hand! He was begging me to let him go. Alice was rolling on the floor in laughter. I learned a valuable principle from that experience. You cannot move forward if you are holding on to a monster behind you

Unresolved issues from your past can kill your ministry. Unresolved relationship issues are one of the most common reasons that young ministers with great potential never have the impact in ministry God intended.

All in the Family

There is no such thing as a perfect family. There are family skeletons in all of our closets that we would rather not deal with. In order to be effective in ministry, however, you need to get the skeletons out of your closet and into the graveyard where they belong. For better or for worse, the way your were raised will affect your ministry. Your orientation family influences how you view the family of God. In particular, your relationship with your biological father can have a telling impact on how you view and relate to God.

Sins of the Fathers

Was your father abusive? How did he treat your mother? How do you feel about your father now? If you are married, can you honestly say that you know how to disagree with your wife without becoming physically or verbally abusive?

One of the scandals of modern Christendom is the fact that there are currently men in our pulpits who physically and emotionally abuse their spouses and children on a regular basis.

The prophets Ezekiel and Jeremiah talk about the fathers eating sour grapes but the children's teeth being set on edge. (Jeremiah 31:29; Ezekiel 18:2) While we don't have space to consider all of the ramifications of transgenerational sin in this book, the point for our discussion is this: If your father expressed his feelings by fussing, cussing, kicking and slapping, you are likely to do the same if you don't make a conscience effort to do something different. Unless you confess and forsake the sins of your father and let the Holy Spirit renew the spirit of your mind through the Word, you are likely to raise a bunch of fussing, cussing, kicking and slapping kids. You can break the cycle in your generation but you have to be willing to admit your problem, submit yourself to God, commit yourself to His word, and seek godly accountability. If you were raised in a family that was either verbally, emotionally, physically or sexually abusive, your view of relationships will be distorted. That distortion will affect your personal relationship as well as your ministry unless and until you allow God to heal you. The healing process cannot begin until you acknowledge your past.

How Does Your Garden Grow?

See to it that no one comes short of the grace of God; that no root of bitterness springing up cause trouble and by it many be defiled.

Hebrews 12:15 (NAU)

Unprocessed experiences from your past can produce negative emotional patterns that grow like weeds on the landscape of your soul. If left unchecked they multiply and choke out the fruit of the Spirit in your life. Weeds cannot be effectively dealt with by chopping off the tops. To deal conclusively with a weed you need to get to its root. The same is true as it relates to the weeds that litter our souls. You must examine the roots of your negative emotions and behaviors.

For example, how do you respond to conflict? Do you become overly defensive when someone disagrees with you? Do you avoid conflict altogether? Do you have an explosive temper? A lot of church conflicts are really about misdirected anger and unresolved issues from home being played out in the congregation. As a minister, you must learn the fine art of self-examination to make sure that unresolved issues from your upbringing do not hinder your present usefulness in the kingdom. Paul told Timothy, *"Take heed unto thyself, and unto the doctrine, continue in them. For by doing this thou shalt both save thyself and them that hear thee." I Timothy 4:16*

Papa was a Rolling Stone

Was your father physically available to you? If not, have you forgiven him for not being there for you? I have known angry young men to go into ministry. Some young men go into ministry hurting and in the process of trying to minister are hurting others. On the other hand, I know young men who have come out of single-parent households who are well-balanced men, loving husbands, conscientious fathers, and effective ministers. The key to success is not what happens to you but how you respond.

Perhaps your father abandoned your family. Maybe your father was physically present but emotionally distant. It could be that you do not know who your father is. Whatever your specific case may be, one thing is certain; your attitude about your father can have a tremendous affect on your ability to minister. Your attitude about your biological father has an effect on how you understand and communicate truths about our Heavenly Father. Unresolved anger or bitterness toward fathers often manifests itself in contortions and misperceptions of the character of God. The last verse in the Old Testament speaks of restoring the hearts of the fathers to their children, and the hearts of the children to their fathers, lest the Lord smite the land with a curse. (Malachi 4:6) Could it be that our society is in the condition it is in because of so many unresolved issues between fathers and children, even children who sit in the pulpit? Part of attaining maturity is acknowledging and accepting the shortcomings of your father. Without forgiving those in your past who have let you down, it is impossible to move forward.

Papa was a Rolling Stone Remix

By the way, are you an absent father? None of use has been saved all of our lives. Some of use sowed many wild oats before we received Christ. Sadly enough, some of us are still sowing even since we have received Christ. It is not just the sowing but the reaping that can kill your ministry. What you sow secretly you might reap publicly. While child support payments, custody orders and visitation agreements are the most obvious burdens of past indiscretion; my concern is the not-so-obvious impact. Do you have minor children who do not live with you? What does it say about your integrity if you preach about a Heavenly Father who meets all your needs but you will not fulfill your financial obligations toward your children without a court order? Isn't there an inherent inconsistency in claiming to represent the One who will never leave us nor forsake us and you will not even visit your children? The issue is one of moral integrity.

Your children need at least three things from you in addition to financial support. God Himself gave us a model in Matthew 3:16-17:

Visible Acknowledgment

> *"And after being baptized, Jesus went up immediately from the water; and behold, the heavens were opened and he saw the Spirit of God descending as a dove, and coming upon him ..."*

Your presence speaks volumes. There is something about the presence of a godly man that brings about a sense of security and confidence. Every child needs to have the reassuring presence of "Daddy" especially at crucial times. A boy needs to be around a man in order to develop his image of what it means to be a man. In order to be a man you have to see a man. A girl needs to be around a man so she can know what to expect from genuine masculinity. If your girl hangs around a real man long enough (assuming that is what you are) then she can easily spot a counterfeit.

Voluntary Affirmation

> *"And behold, a voice out of the heavens, saying, 'This is my beloved Son,"*

God publicly declared his love for Jesus before he started his ministry. This declaration of love was based on their relationship and not on performance. Jesus had not done anything yet. Do not make your children wrestle for a blessing. Affirmation that is not voluntary is destructive.

Vocal Approval

"in whom I am well pleased."

God said out loud, "He makes me happy." Never underestimate the power your words have on your children. Proverbs 16:24 says, *"Pleasant words are as an honey comb; sweet to the soul and health to the bones."* Proverbs 18:21 says, *"Death and life are in the power of the tongue."* Your vocal approval can motivate your child in unbelievable ways. Remember, we are working so that one day we will hear Jesus say, "Well done, thou good and faithful servant."

The Ties that Blind

If you are married can you honestly say that you have severed all of your past romantic relationships? A man was sitting on his couch watching TV when his wife came up behind him and hit him on the head with a rolled up newspaper. "What was that for?" he asked in exasperation. "I found a piece of paper in your jacket with some numbers and the name Mary Lou on it! Are you cheating on me?" his wife asked. "Of course not, sweetheart. Mary Lou is the name of a horse I bet on the other day at the track. Those numbers were just the odds." That seemed to satisfy the wife until the next evening when she answered the phone. After she hung up, she got a skillet and cracked her husband on the head again. When he regained consciousness he stammered, "Now what was that for?" to which the wife replied "That was your horse on the phone. She won't be able to make it tonight!" What are you going to do when your "Mary Lou" shows up?

If you have been physically intimate with someone of the opposite sex to whom you were not married, you must take care to make sure your soul is not still tied to theirs if you want to minister effectively. I once witnessed a minister take his text, start the introduction to his sermon, and then stop dead in his tracks because a particular woman walked into the room. He could not go on with his sermon because this woman sat directly in front of him and they had some ongoing sexual issues that were hampering his witness. I have seen others jeopardize their marriage because some "Mary Lou" from the past came calling and the brother did not know how to handle it.

The Bible says that sexual intercourse is like superglue.

> *There's more to sex than mere skin on skin. Sex is as much spiritual mystery as physical fact. As written in Scripture, "The two become one."*
>
> I CORINTHIANS 6:16 (MSG)

If you are still stuck on "Mary Lou" then get help immediately. Seek godly counsel and accountability. Admit your feelings to God and another mature Christian or a group of Christians who can pray with you and help your work through your emotions. But whatever you do, let go of "Mary Lou." She might be the monster that is keeping you from progressing in ministry.

Chapter 11

Temple Prostitutes
The Male Associate Minister and Sexuality

Throughout history, there has always been an uneasy connection between religious activities and sexual excitement. In Old Testament times, the Canaanites had temple prostitutes. Israel was warned not to associate with that practice or the money it generated:

> *There shall be no whore of the daughters of Israel, nor a sodomite of the sons of Israel. Thou shalt not bring the hire of a whore, or the price of a dog (male temple prostitute), into the house of the LORD thy God for any vow: for even both these are abomination unto the LORD thy God.*
>
> Deuteronomy 23:17-18 (KJV)

In the New Testament, Paul warned the Corinthian church about the dangers of dabbling in goddess worship because it was fraught with temple prostitution. (I Corinthians 10) Today's headlines testify that sexual promiscuity is affecting ministers and ministry in a devastating way. In the spring of 1999, the Dean of Harvard Divinity School was forced to resign because they found pornographic material on his school-owned computer. The President of the National Baptist Convention, USA, Inc., resigned amidst allegations of extramarital impropriety. Former President Clinton's affair with Monica Lewinsky shows that even the most powerful man in the free world is not immune from sexual temptation. Rev. Jesse Jackson counseled former President Clinton only to admit later that he had fathered a child out of wedlock around the same time as the scandal was taking place. As I write these words, Kobe Bryant is facing rape charges that if proven could end his career. Over the years, many famous men and great men of God have sacrificed their reputations, their ministries and their families on the altar of sexual immorality.

Saved But Not Superman

Some ministers think that they are impervious to sexual temptation. A minister must be in touch with his own humanity. Just because you can parse Greek and Hebrew and can move people homiletically does not mean that you are above being tempted by the flesh. Furthermore, proficiency in the spiritual disciplines does not kill God-given desires and needs. Spiritual disciplines like prayer, fasting, solitude, and bible study help us to train our hearts and minds to keep our desires and needs in the proper context. Nevertheless, you must always remember God made you a sexual being. One of the implications of being a sexual being is that you will be attracted to the opposite sex. Though the intensity of sexual urges may diminish with age, they never completely go away.

Sexual attraction and appreciation is God-given and, therefore, not sinful. The issue is keeping it in its proper context and within the confines of scriptural limits. Fire kept within the context of a fireplace is romantic, warmth giving, and a thing of beauty. When that same fire exceed the limits of the fireplace and get into the curtains, the furniture and the woodwork, it becomes destructive, consuming and a thing of horror. The same is true for the minister's sexuality. When its expression is kept within scriptural limits and a godly context, it is beautiful and life affirming. Out of the proper context it is as ugly as sin because it is just that; sin.

The Favor of God and the Effect of the Annointing

You must always be mindful of the attractive nature of the anointing. The presence of the Holy Spirit in a person's life often makes that person attractive to the opposite sex. Misunderstanding in this area can derail your ministry before it ever picks up speed. If the Lord has placed a special calling or anointing on your life there is a strong likelihood that women will find you emotionally and potentially sexually attractive. "So what?" you might ask. The problem is that the level of sexual frustration in the contemporary church is enormously high. Many Christian women have all but given up hope of finding a godly man to show them attention. When you exclude the brothers in the criminal justice system, those on drugs, those who are homosexual or bisexual, and those who have three or four sets of children by different women, there are not many brothers left to count. Of the ones that don't fit into any of the categories above, how many of them would you say love God, have a job, and are willing to love a woman like Christ loves the church?

Now you understand the tremendous pressure and frustration that many single Christian women face. That is why when they see you on Sunday, a righteous man who speaks with authority and has all of his teeth, you might appear to be attractive. Most women, whether consciously or unconsciously, admire men of authority, power, passion and creativity. Who possesses all of these qualities in greater abundance than a Spirit-filled man of God?

Depending upon the woman and her circumstances this natural admiration can turn into a consuming sexual attraction. Just ask Joseph. According to Genesis 39:2, "The Lord was with Joseph." There was a special calling on his life. Joseph was successful even while a slave and later a prisoner because of God's favor. That same anointing made him attractive to Potiphar's wife. The fact that he was handsome and well built as well as creative made him irresistible as far as Mrs. Potiphar was concerned. By the grace of God, Joseph had the spiritual fortitude to resist her advances and the wisdom to flee when it got too hot in the kitchen.

What will you do when your time comes? What are you going to do when that sister tries to put a little something extra in that hug after church? What are you going to do when that beautiful but frustrated married woman invites you to come to a secluded place so that you can give her "spiritual guidance" in a private setting? What are you going to do when that single sister keeps finding ways to get involved in every ministry and class you are involved in and finds excuses to call you about "church business" at odd hours of the night? What are you going to do when a sister flat out tells you what she wants, how she wants it and she won't take "no" for an answer? Do not wait until it happens. Strategize now.

Here are some suggested safeguards and responses:

Run for your life!

Book! Jet! Break camp! Raise up! Get ghost! Make like a banana and split! However you translate the biblical imperative to "flee" the point is to leave the source of sexual temptation as soon as possible. Sexual immorality and youthful lusts are not to be fought in the usual sense of the word. The Bible tells us in explicit terms to flee both of these. (I Corinthians 6:19, II Timothy 2:22) God has an escape hatch for every temptation. (I Corinthians 10:13) As it relates to sexual temptation the sooner you run from the source, the better off you will be.

If the sister is after you, or if you feel a strong attraction to her, do not linger with your eye contact or listen to her voice too long. Proverbs 6:25 says, *"Do not desire her beauty in your heart, nor let her catch you with her eyelids."* Proverbs 5:3 says, *"For the lips of an adulteress drip honey, and smoother than oil is her speech; but in the end she is bitter as wormwood, sharp as a two-edged sword."* If you are close enough to be intoxicated by her perfume, you are too close. If you stay in her presence too long you will yield. Therefore, do not put yourself in that position. Stay away from settings that would even appear to be compromising. If you honestly do not want to eat the forbidden fruit, then stop swinging on the tree. Something just might fall in your lap.

Trust the instincts of your closest female relative

If you are married and in the ministry, you need to listen to your wife. If your wife says that she does not trust someone or that Sis. So-and-So has impure intentions, you should take heed. God has given you a helper for a reason; you need help! Women know more about other women than men will ever know. Women pay attention to details. They notice each other's vibes and moods. They can decipher what certain gestures, eye movements, and vocal cues mean. Your wife is your greatest ally, therefore you must learn to listen to her even if you cannot see what she is saying. Just because you are not attracted to another woman does not mean that the woman is not attracted to you and waiting to lay a trap. If your wife tells you that a particular person seems to have a problem speaking to her, yet that same person is always in your face, take note. Your wife's instincts are worth trusting.

If you are not married and have no female relatives at your church, then you should adopt some spiritual mothers. I have found it useful before and since I got married to have a spiritual older woman in my life who has "got my back." Spiritual older women know how to keep younger women in check and they know how to check you if you get out of line. Our Church Concierge has an office right outside of mine. She is a seasoned saint who has raised children, grandchildren and great-grandchildren. One day I was explaining to a visitor that our Church Concierge is somewhat of a gatekeeper for the church. "She watches out for the wolves," I quipped. She quickly retorted, "Yeah, and the foxes too!" Foxes can cause just as much if not more damage than wolves if left unchecked. Enlist the elder saints to watch your back and to check your canine propensities.

Treat Her Like Your Sister

The women in our churches are not playthings. They are not just a collection of pretty faces and body parts. They are our sisters, mothers and daughters. First Timothy 5:2 says we ought to treat younger women like sisters, "in all purity." "In all purity" means with unpolluted motives.

In other words, make sure that as you deal with that sister, the words of your mouth and the meditations of your heart are acceptable in His sight. Why? Because she is your sister. How would you want your biological sister to be treated? Would you want someone to take advantage of your sister? Would you want another minister to play with your sister's emotions in order to stroke his own ego? If a woman that you are not married to is attracted to you, remember that not only is she your sister but she has an Elder Brother who doesn't take kindly to people misusing His little sisters.

Watch Yourself

Do you have a flirtatious spirit? Are there certain things you say and certain mannerisms you display when you are around attractive women that could be looked at by others as if you were using poor judgment? Are you friendly to everyone or just to women who fit a certain profile?

Do your speech patterns befit your temperament, your age, and the culture in which you live? I grew up in a small Midwestern city called Kankakee. The pace is slow and most of the African Americans who live there are from Mississippi. The church family there is close-knit and family oriented. All of the older people call the younger people "baby" or some equally affectionate nickname. I am a people person by nature and got into the habit of addressing any woman that was younger than me as "baby." When I moved to Oakland, California and got married, I moved into a completely different culture. I was still calling all the younger women "baby" when my wife pulled me aside and let me know that I was not in Kankakee anymore! In Oakland's culture, I was not old enough to use "baby" as a term of endearment. What was considered friendly in Kankakee was considered flirtatious in Oakland.

Similarly, I have had to learn how to watch my mannerisms. I do not give full body hugs to sisters I am not related to. I hug sisters by either putting my arm around their shoulder and bringing them to my side or by holding their hand in a handshake posture and patting them on the back with the other hand. In general, I only kiss the older ladies and only on the cheek at that.

When I teach in small settings, I tend to touch my student's on the shoulder or make direct eye contact with a specific student to make a point. After watching me in a few settings my wife perceived that my actions were communicating something I did not intend them to communicate to some of the sisters, so I changed my style. I still hug and shake hands and laugh and joke because that is my nature. I also take heed to myself lest my good be spoken evil of.

Set up personal boundaries

Some habits are worth developing because they set up boundaries that will protect you when you are weak. If you become known for a certain pattern of behavior, it can help quash some lies before they get started. Some simple habits I have developed have proven to be helpful to me.

- ✓ Whenever I am traveling alone I disable the adult movie channels in my hotel room or unplug the TV altogether. Why? I do not plan to watch much television and I definitely do not plan to watch any pornography so why even have the temptation available?
- ✓ I keep a picture of my wife and children at the office and in my wallet at all times. Why? In case I am tempted to flirt or someone flirts with me. I can pull out the pictures and close that door of opportunity.

- ✓ I let my wife know my schedule whether I am at home or abroad so that she can reach me twenty-four hours a day. Why? I don't plan to do anything wrong so why shouldn't she know exactly where I am going and what I am doing?
- ✓ If a woman comes to my office for a meeting I never close the door all the way or meet when there is no one else in the building. Why? I do not plan to do anything unseemly and I do not want to be falsely accused of having done so.
- ✓ I let my wife know if I am meeting with another sister be it for ministry business or spiritual guidance. Why? So my wife can monitor my level of contact with a person and help me keep an above-board approach to relationships.
- ✓ I do not befriend or maintain friendships with women with whom my wife is not comfortable. Why? I promised to forsake all others in deference to her. Why would I need a female friend that she does not like?

Set up your own personal boundaries according to your specific situation. It will help you keep a clear conscience. Even if people lie on you, your pattern of good behavior will be so obvious that the slanderers will be put to shame. (I Peter 3:16)

Don't Isolate Yourself

Take a lesson from the life of David. While Jonathan was alive David had a godly accountability partner. When he was discouraged and under tremendous pressure, Jonathan would strengthen his hand in the Lord. (I Samuel 23:16) After Jonathan died, David did not find anyone to take his place. The record states:

> *In the spring, at the time when kings go off to war, David sent Joab out with the king's men and the whole Israelite army. They destroyed the Ammonites and besieged Rabbah. But David remained in Jerusalem.*
>
> 2 SAM 11:1 (NIV)

You know the rest of the story. While all the men were off doing what they were supposed to do, this isolated king became a voyeur, an adulterer, a liar, and a murderer. Isolation can lead you to impure fantasies. Fantasy left unchecked can develop into full-blown lust. Lust once it has been impregnated by opportunity will give birth to sin. Sin ultimately gives birth to death. (James 1:15)

I have some godly men in my life that I check in with on almost a daily basis. These brothers can tell when something is wrong with me even if I do not articulate it. We pray for one another and share each other's struggles. I have to admit there are some stupid things I probably would have seriously considered doing if not for the fact that later on that day I was going to have to talk to one of my brothers and they were going to question me about my walk.

Renew Your Mind

Did you become sexually active at a young age? If you did it probably has had an impact on how you view women in general. For many males in our society "manhood" is defined and calibrated by the number of female sexual conquests. Unfortunately, that attitude has entrenched itself into certain circles of the clergy. If your sense of manhood is tied into how many sexual partners you have had, you need to rethink the biblical definition of manhood.

We must train our minds to think of women in terms of personality rather than body parts. That is not to say that you have sinned if you notice a shapely woman. You cannot always control what comes into your plane of view. You can control what you focus on and what you replay in your mind. The issue is what you meditate on. As one theologian put it, "We cannot keep birds from flying over our heads but we can keep them from building nests in our hair." Jesus said that a man that looks upon a woman for the purpose of lusting after her has committed adultery in his heart already. Contemporary media makes it easy to commit "heart adultery." From the subtle sexual innuendoes of advertisers to the explicit pull of pornographic websites, we have the opportunity to sin in this area almost daily. That is why we must discipline our hearts and minds by *"taking every thought captive unto the obedience of Jesus Christ." (II Corinthians 10:4,5)*

Guard your heart

Ministry is first and foremost an inside job. That is why the proverb writer would say, *"Watch over your heart with all diligence, for from it flow the springs of life."* Proverbs 4:23 Jesus said, *"The good man brings good things out of the good stored up in him, and the evil man brings evil things out of the evil stored up in him."* Matt. 12:35

An effective minister must guard his heart at all times. The enemy will do all he can to impregnate your heart with the seeds of discouragement, disillusion and disappointment. To medicate our hurts Satan and society offer the lust of the flesh, the lust of the eyes and the pride of life. Jesus Christ offers to heal us with His love, fortify us with hope and make us whole through faith in His completed work on Calvary.

Other Stuff That We Don't Like to Talk About

There are many internal affairs that demand our diligent vigilance. Some issues are more prevalent in today's society than they were in previous generations. Ironically, the church has been largely silent on some of the more glaring vices. Perhaps one of the reasons is that we as ministers are afraid to confront our own humanity. By remaining silent on our own pet sins we have allowed those pets to grow up to be the predators that are devouring our testimonies, ministries and marriages. As one young man aptly stated, "It's the stuff we don't like to talk about that's killing us."

Dogs and Cats

Satan often ensnares us by either exploiting our weaknesses or pushing our strengths out of context. Passion, creativity and the ability to connect emotionally with people are gifts that are usually resident in a God-called preacher. These same attributes can be the seeds of your own destruction if allowed to grow outside of the garden of godly accountability. Examine these subtle weeds that have the potential of marring the landscapes of our souls.

Cell Phone Sex

I am not referring here to using your cell phone to dial up some charge by the minute "talk-dirty-to-me" phone service. I am pointing out that the cell phone has changed the way we communicate. Undisciplined cell phone usage can make you available to be tempted 24 hours a day. If you are undisciplined in who you give your number to and to whom you talk on a regular basis, you can set yourself up for an affair via the airwaves. You do not have to engage in intercourse to be inappropriately intimate with someone. You can develop a soul tie with whomever you share intimate information with if you spend enough time with them. The cell phone makes it possible to be in constant communication with someone even though you are not physically in their presence. Use your minutes wisely. Overusage could not only be a signal that you are talking too much but might be telling you that you are talking too much to the wrong person.

Internet Sex

Internet chat rooms, instant messaging and internet pornography have exponentially expanded the opportunities to sin for those who choose to do so. The anonymity that the internet affords is a deadly trap to the undisciplined and secluded soul. The internet has become one of the newest addictions. Pornographic sites are by far the most downloaded sites on the web. If you are currently ensnared by the dark side of the web, please take drastic action. There are several excellent but inexpensive internet filters on the market right now. There are also some Christian websites that have free tools and resources to aid you in your fight for purity. Set some boundaries for yourself. Do not engage in chat room conversations that would be viewed as inappropriate if the language was spoken. Keep track of when and how long you stay on line. Do not surf aimlessly. If you are not looking for specific information then log off and find something more productive to do.

Emotional Adultery

It is possible to commit adultery with engaging in physical intercourse. Emotional adultery is more insidious than a one night stand because the participants in an emotional affair actually believe that they are in love.

Never share information with another woman that would embarrass your wife or devalue her in the eyes of the listener. If you are having problems in your marriage then you need to find a godly brother or godly married couple to talk to. When you share intimate information (i.e., fears, frustrations, dreams, fantasies) with a woman other than your wife you automatically create a bond that God did not intend to be forged. Similarly, be careful about how much information you allow someone to share with you. Many an illegitimate relationship has developed on the basis of a legitimate sharing situation that went too far.

Convention Affairs

I have not attended every state or national meeting of every different denomination but I have close friends in each denomination who have. Whether you call it convention, convocation, congress, general assembly or annual meeting there will always be a small group of ministers who attend a meeting so they can release their tension in inappropriate ways. Unfortunately, there tend to be "gospel groupies" at most denominational meetings who come for no other reason than to be the tension relievers for the aforementioned group. There is nothing inherently evil about denominational meetings. But remember whenever there is a large crowd of people there will always be mixed motives in the multitude. Some will be there to learn and grow. Others will be there to explore the night life of the host city and the amenities their fellow convention delegate's hotel rooms. If you go to the meeting, then represent your Christ and your church with dignity. Do not get caught up in a night of passion that can give you a lifetime of pain and 18 years of child support.

Fleecing the Flock

The sisters in your congregation ought to be able to look to you as a protector not a predator. The unfortunate reality is that some associate ministers mar their ministry before it gets started well because they systematically defraud and deflower the sisters in the congregation. If you mess up any where it will eventually catch up to you. But when you mess up at home the consequences and repercussions are more immediate and intense. Taking advantage of those you are supposed to help shepherd will get you in trouble with the Lord and the law. Do not use your popularity as a preacher or your status as a son of the ministry to excuse your promiscuous behavior or to financially abuse the membership. I have known gifted ministers who used their status and power of persuasion to dupe unsuspecting women into giving them clothes, cars and cash. The devastation that it causes in an individual sister's life and the lives of her family, if they belong to the church, can have a ripple effect through the entire congregation and community.

What about your bark?

Dogs ought to bark. Cats ought to meow. There is a cartoon that is popular among children today called "Cat-Dog." It chronicles the exploits of an animal that is half cat and half dog. Cat-Dog barks and meows. Cat-Dog is a fictional character. Unfortunately, "cat-dogitis" is growing amongst the ranks of popular pulpiteers in America. The homosexual and bisexual exploits of prominent pastors has become standard scuttlebutt in certain circles. Anecdotal evidence suggests that the current strategy is to recruit young, gifted preachers, woo them with friendship and preaching opportunities and them "turn them out". The built in secrecy is predicated on embarrassment. Those who engage in such behavior do not necessarily consider themselves homosexual though the acts fit the biblical definition.

Do not trade in your bark!

No amount of money, popularity or prestige is worth trading in God's purpose, plan and design for your sexuality. If something happened in your past that has caused you to be attracted to men or if some relationship you experimented with went too far there is still hope. God has a designed you to be a man for a reason. When you choose to rebel against His design and plan for your masculinity you also frustrate His purpose for your life. Bring your situation to light in the confines of a godly pastor or Christian counselor and let God fulfill His purpose through you the way He planned and designed it.

Action Points *Keeping It Real*

These questions are for you and your accountability partner.

- ❑ Would Jesus Christ be pleased if He reviewed your cell phone record and the transcripts of your conversations on the cell phone? Would your wife/fiancée/girlfriend/mother be pleased?

- ❑ Would Jesus Christ be pleased if He reviewed the log of the Internet sites you have visited recently or looked in on your chat room conversations? Would your wife/fiancée/girlfriend/mother be pleased?

- ❏ Is there someone in your life that you share an illegitimate soul tie with? How did that soul tie develop?

- ❏ Are you participating in a sexual affair right now?

- ❏ When are you most tempted to violate God's principles in this area?

- ❏ Who or what helped you to formulate your views on women?

Here are three things I covenant to do this week in order to keep my mind pure and to shun the very appearance of evil:

1.

2.

3.

POSTSCRIPT

Sex immorality is not the only area that can trip a minister up. Illegal drugs, alcohol and legal substance abuse are equally as deadly and prevalent. The bottom line to keeping your spirit inoculated against any of these insidious vices is to keep your soul fed. *"The full soul loatheth an honeycomb; but to the hungry soul every bitter thing is sweet." Proverb 27:7* The Living Bible renders that same verse, *"Even honey seems tasteless to a man who is full; but if he is hungry, he'll eat anything!"*

List here the top three ways that you can keep your soul full so that you won't be tempted to nibble on illicit sex, drugs, alcohol or overeating.

1.

2.

3.

Chapter 12

Silver and Gold Have I None

My father used to say, "Son, if you're going to be in full-time ministry, you've got to learn how to live poor."

One skill that you must learn is the art of living without. You do not have to be poor in order to be an effective minister. An effective minister must learn, however, the secret of contentment. The apostle Paul stated:

> *I have learned, in whatsoever state I am, therewith to be content. I know both how to be abased, and I know how to abound: every where and in all things I am instructed both to be full and to be hungry, both to abound and to suffer need.*
>
> Philippians 4:11(b)-12 (KJV)

There is nothing inherently wrong with possessing material wealth. Nevertheless, your attitude about money can definitely determine your usefulness to the kingdom.

The mistake many of us make is we try to "be big" before we "get big." A minister who has not learned how to be content regardless of his circumstances is likely to spend unnecessary energy trying to maintain a certain "image" or "profile". Some of us go into the ministry thinking that we are automatically entitled to the honor and honorariums that it took seasoned pastors decades to earn.

Many people have a misguided notion of what type of clothes a minister should wear, what type of car he should drive, and the overall persona that he should project. Unfortunately, these preconceived notions rarely have any biblical basis. If the image in your mind of a successful minister primarily centers on clothes, cars and cash then you will constantly be comparing your present situation with that illusive image. Comparison always leads to competition. When the neophyte minister compares himself with either his preconceived image or the cultural stereotype of ministers, the temptation to compete with that image or stereotype can be powerful. The temptation to compete is often the fiercest at conventions, congress, convocations, conferences and other gatherings where a large number of ministers are present.

A few years ago, I attended the national meeting of a large Christian group. I decided to go to a late night service in order to support the minister who was scheduled to preach that night. I sat down next to a young lady who had apparently been around a lot of ministers. While I was trying to worship, I noticed that she was looking at what I was wearing with an obvious attitude of disapproval. "You call yourself a preacher dressed like that?" she asked. Somewhat befuddled, I checked my clothing to see if something was out of place. I was wearing newly polished black shoes, black socks, a dark blue pinstriped suit, freshly pressed white shirt and a tie with a dark blue and purple pattern in it. "What's wrong?" I asked. "Well, you don't even have a pocket silk with matching suspenders!" she replied. Before I responded, I scanned the large ballroom where we were seated. Many of the prominent preachers were wearing bright yellow, orange, red, purple, green, and yes, even pink suits. Some were wearing matching alligator shoes and most were wearing ties with matching pockets silks and suspenders. The atmosphere was almost like a fashion show. I was one of the most conservatively dressed ministers in the room. As one popular preacher walked in wearing a bright orange suit with bright orange alligator shoes and what appeared to be a fur pocket silk, I told the young lady, "I guess you're right, I must not be much of a preacher if that's what preaching is about!"

Dangerous Debt

Some ministers acquire a tremendous amount of debt by trying to keep up with the latest fashions or driving the most expensive cars they can afford. Debt is a harsh taskmaster and it often tempts us to compromise our convictions. When I was just starting out in ministry, a local pastor invited me to do a youth revival at his church. I was excited about this opportunity and shared the good news with one of my peers, a young preacher at the church I attended. "I don't do revivals," my friend explained, "because they don't do any good. You go preach for a week to a group of strangers and then when you leave they go back to doing what they were doing before you came." He then proceeded to give me several theological-sounding arguments and scriptures to back up his premise. "I'll never do a revival," he declared. Less than a year later my colleague's money started getting funny. Guess what he started doing all over the city? You guessed it! Revivals! I learned two important lessons from that experience:

1. Never say "never".
2. Financial pressure can shape your convictions if you let it.

Whether you are just starting out in ministry, are already a full-time staff minister, or a non-salaried associate minister, your attitude about money can either frustrate or fortify your effectiveness in ministry. Allow me to remind you of a few simple truths about ministry and money.

GOD HAS PROMISED TO SUPPLY ALL OF YOUR NEEDS NOT ALL OF YOUR GREEDS.

Scripture guarantees us that we will have everything we need in order to fulfill God's purpose in our lives. Scripture does not guarantee that we will have everything we want. The fact that God does not always give us what we want is one of the most profound manifestations of His love for us. No loving parent would give his or her children everything they asked for because children always want candy and toys but seldom want what is most beneficial for their growth and development. We all have asked God for things that we thought we wanted at the time only to find out later that had He granted our request we would be miserable. If we make His kingdom and His righteousness our priority, He will give us what we need in order to get the job done.

FAITHFULNESS DOES NOT GUARANTEE THAT YOU WILL NEVER BE BROKE.

Throughout history, God has proven that He can take care of His messenger without the assistance of traditional avenues of revenue. In other words, God can and will take care of you whether you have money in your pocket or not. He has the ability to sustain you with or without a job. The size of your bank account is not necessarily an accurate indicator of God's favor in your life. It is possible to be broke and blessed or wealthy and wicked. It is also possible to be broke and wicked or blessed and wealthy. My point is that your conscientious service to the kingdom does not guarantee that you will never suffer material want. The Believer's Hall of Fame, recorded in Hebrews chapter 11, lists people who:

> *wandered about in sheepskins and goatskins; being* ***destitute****, afflicted, and tormented; of whom the world was not worthy: they wandered in deserts, and in mountains, and in dens and caves of the earth. And all these, having obtained a good report through faith, received not the promise.*
>
> HEBREWS 11:37B-39(KJV)

The apostle Paul stated that although his ministry was approved by God, he had to minister *"in much patience, in affliction, in* ***necessities,*** *in distresses . . . as poor, yet making many rich; as having nothing and yet possessing all things." II Corinthians 6:4,10 (KJV)*

There are several reasons that you might have seasons of material scarcity during your ministry.

Bad financial decisions from the past

"God is not mocked; whatsoever a man soweth that shall he also reap." Galatians 6:6 (KJV) Debt is just like body fat. It takes much longer to get rid of it than it did to get it. Sometimes you do not have enough today because of what you did yesterday.

Living beyond your means

Just because you see it does not mean you need it. Just because they extend you credit does not mean you should buy it. Credit card debt is a form of slavery. *"The rich ruleth over the poor, and the borrower is servant to the lender." Proverbs 22:7 (KJV)* Credit cards are shackles. A platinum shackle is still a shackle. Learn to use credit wisely if at all. If you have not planned for it in your budget and you cannot pay cash for it, then you probably do not need it.

Not planning for emergencies

People get sick. Cars break down. You will eventually have to funeralize a close relative. It is foolish not to prepare for the contingencies of life that eventually affect us all. *"A sensible man watches for problems ahead and prepares to meet them. The simpleton never looks and suffers the consequences." Proverbs 27:12(TLB)*

A call to full-time ministry

The call to the preaching ministry is not necessarily a call to quit your secular job. If God makes provision for you to go into full-time ministry, be mindful that the average church cannot compete with corporate America in terms of salary. Full-time ministry usually requires a sacrifice of salary initially when compared to the secular world. Nevertheless, God has some fringe benefits that will more than make up the difference.

A spouse that does not share your values

If you and your spouse are not equally yoked, as it relates to your attitude about finances, chances are there will not only be conflict in the home but also a perpetual lack of money. If one or the other of you is greedy, covetous, materialistic, or overly image-conscious, there will never be enough money in the household. *"He that loveth silver shall not be satisfied with silver; nor he that loveth abundance with increase: this is also vanity." Ecclesiastes 5:10(KJV)*

Not following a written spending plan

If you do not carefully manage your resources by following a budget, chances are you will waste the bulk of your money on impulse spending. There is a whole industry built on the premise that people can be persuaded to buy products they do not need if they are repeatedly exposed to the product by the artful use of images, music and catchy slogans. Marketing strategist, advertisers and television producers owe the billions of dollars they make each year to the undeniable fact that they can make most people want their product even though they probably do not need it.

The Sovereignty of God

Sometimes you do everything right and you still come up short. Be mindful of the fact that God's thoughts are not our thoughts and His ways are not our ways. Job suffered through a season of tremendous loss though he was a perfect and upright man. Sometimes we go through seasons of drought for reasons we will never fully understand while we live down here. We can rest in the assurance that God has a plan even when we do not understand. *"'For I know the plans I have for you,' declares the LORD, 'plans to prosper you and not to harm you, plans to give you hope and a future.'" Jeremiah 29:11(NIV)*

Pay Day Afterwhile

God has promised that we will receive whatever is right. There is a parable recorded in Matthew chapter 20 that emphasizes my initial point about the folly of comparison when it comes to kingdom benefits. Jesus told this parable in response to Peter's question as to what he and the rest of the disciples would receive for forsaking all to follow Him. (Matthew 19:27) Jesus said that a landowner went out early in the morning to hire some laborers to work in his vineyard. He negotiated with the first group of laborers he met and hired them after they settled on the customary pay for a full day's work. Throughout the remainder of the day this same landowner met others idly standing by and immediately sent them to his vineyard promising to pay whatever was right. When quitting time came, he called the laborers he had hired last to receive their pay first. Ultimately, the laborers who had worked for an hour received the same pay as those who had worked for twelve hours. Those who had worked the longest started complaining. However, the landowner replied "I gave you exactly what you contracted for. I can do what I want with what belongs to me. These other men went out into the field without a written contract and trusted the promise that I would do what was right." This parable places before us some sobering questions:

1. Am I willing to be faithful to my calling regardless of the pay?
2. Do I need a contract before I can go to work in His vineyard or can I trust Him to do what is right?
3. Do I get jealous if I see others being blessed although I have worked harder and longer than they have?

The next time you are tempted to complain remember that there are ministers in other parts of His vineyard who work twice as hard as you do, receive half the pay, and are ten times more grateful to God.

Distracted, Deceived and Drowning

Jesus said that the cares of this world and the deceitfulness of riches can strangle the word in your life and make you unfruitful. (Matthew 13:22) Anxiety about material abundance is a deadly distraction. Remember Paul's warning to Timothy:

> *These arguers— their minds warped by sin— don't know how to tell the truth; to them the Good News is just a means of making money. Keep away from them. Do you want to be truly rich? You already are if you are happy and good. After all, we didn't bring any money with us when we came into the world, and we can't carry away a single penny when we die. So we should be well satisfied without money if we have enough food and clothing. But people who long to*

> *be rich soon begin to do all kinds of wrong things to get money, things that hurt them and make them evil-minded and finally send them to hell itself. For the love of money is the first step toward all kinds of sin. Some people have even turned away from God because of their love for it, and as a result have pierced themselves with many sorrows.*
>
> I TIMOTHY 6:5-10(TLB)

Unfortunately, some people view the preaching ministry as a quick and easy way to get rich. Popular American theology has helped to fuel this spirit of greed by filling the airwaves with promises of material wealth and prosperity to those who "sow seed" (i.e., give money) into particular ministries. As ministers, we must be careful not to get caught up in the spirit of this age. Material gain does not necessarily equal godliness, but godliness with contentment is great gain. (I Timothy 6:6)

CONTENTMENT IS AN ATTITUDE THAT CAN BE LEARNED

Paul said that he learned to be content. Contentment in every circumstance is not automatic. It is something that develops as we mature in Christ and gain His perspective on what is actually happening in our lives. We have to take captive stray thoughts, lest we get caught up in the cheap thrills of this world that often bind us economically. *"Let your conversation be without covetousness; and be content with such things as ye have: for he hath said, I will never leave thee, nor forsake thee." Hebrews 13:5 (KJV)*

Contentment is the key word. Contentment is that frame of mind wherein we are satisfied that what we have been allotted by God is sufficient for us to fulfill His purpose in our lives. Contentment is developed over time. It is a learned attitude. From a prison cell the apostle Paul wrote a thank you letter to the church at Philippi that was brimming with joy. Toward the end of that letter, he states that he had learned how to be content regardless of his circumstances. His contentment was not based on what he had or where he was. Through the enabling power of Christ, he was able to live in the dynamic tension of suffering physical lack yet abounding, of being hungry yet full. An effective minister must learn to cultivate and maintain that same frame of mind.

A Deadly Duo

The opposite of contentment is a pair of sins that seldom are mentioned, but are running rampant in Christendom; greed and covetousness. Greed is a desire to have more than what God has allotted. Covetousness carries with it the connotation of not only wanting more than has been given, but specifically desiring what another has been given. Not only am I dissatisfied with the house God has blessed me with, I want your house.

Covetousness appears to be a harmless sin, but it has the potential to derail your ministry, dilute your message and destroy your marriage. When God prohibited covetousness in the tenth commandment, He was not just adding something to fill out the tablet. Covetousness seriously affects our relationship with God and others. The desire to have more usually results from us comparing ourselves to others. Once you start comparing, you will start competing. Competition and its daughter, Envy, ultimately lead to complaining. This downward spiral of negative attitudes eventually corrodes the soul.

The biblical word for this phenomenon is "fretting." To fret means to feel or express worry, annoyance, discontentment, to become eaten, worn, or corroded. The psalmist admonishes us not to fret ourselves because of evil doers (Don't compare); neither be thou envious (Don't compete), trust in the Lord, delight in him, let him handle your situation, rest in him (Don't complain); cease from anger (Don't corrode). (*paraphrase mine*)

An effective minister must not be greedy for money. (I Timothy 3:3) God has promised that we will receive whatever is right. (Matthew 20:4,14)

Action Points *Fiscally speaking*

- ❑ If a rich benefactor told you that he would pay off all of your debt if you told him how much you owed, would you be able to tell him an exact figure?
- ❑ If you are married, who is better at handling the finances, you or your spouse?
- ❑ When are you most like to make waste money?
- ❑ What is the wisest financial decision you have made recently?
- ❑ How much do you have in savings?

Chapter 13

First Things First: Balancing Home, Ministry and Work

One of the most challenging aspects of being a minister is not the actual ministry you do but prioritizing your time in the face of conflicting obligations and responsibilities. There is no debate that we must seek the kingdom first in all that we do. (Matthew 6:33) Nevertheless, if I am married, have children and a full-time job, how do I maintain a balanced schedule and yet fulfill my duties as a minister? Your time is like money. Mismanagement of either can have a devastating impact on your ministry. Both your budget and your calendar should be critically reviewed and adjusted on a regular basis. A balanced schedule is just as important as a balanced checkbook.

Ministry Begins At Home

Ministry begins at home and spreads abroad. If you are married, your first responsibility is to minister to your spouse. Other than God himself, no one or nothing should have higher priority in your schedule than your spouse. Once you say "I do", you give up the right to make unilateral decisions without considering input from and the impact on your spouse. In particular, a man who will not be considerate of his wife is in danger of arresting his prayer life:

> *Husbands, in the same way be considerate as you live with your wives, and treat them with respect as the weaker partner and as heirs with you of the gracious gift of life, so that nothing will hinder your prayers.*
>
> 1 PETER 3:7 (NIV)

It is tempting to put your spouse on the backburner of your schedule for the sake of ministry. However, be warned; if your relationships are raggedy your ministry will be affected in the long run. You might get by on your giftedness for a season, but eventually the issues of home will manifest themselves in public. One frustrated spouse can tear up a whole church.

That is not to say that you should let your spouse hold your ministry or your joy hostage. You can still have a good marriage even if your spouse has a bad attitude. Of course, it is much harder to live with someone who is contrary but you can still experience joy. If that were not the case then God needs to revise all of the scriptures that admonition us to rejoice and give thanks in every situation. (e.g., Philippians 4:4; 1 Thessalonians 5:16, 18) The issue is not how your spouse acts but how you respond.

The Bible speaks distinctly about a man's responsibility to his wife:

> *And you husbands must love your wives with the same love Christ showed the church. He*

> *gave up his life for her to make her holy and clean, washed by baptism and God's word. He did this to present her to himself as a glorious church without a spot or wrinkle or any other blemish. Instead, she will be holy and without fault. In the same way, husbands ought to love their wives as they love their own bodies. For a man is actually loving himself when he loves his wife. No one hates his own body but lovingly cares for it, just as Christ cares for his body, which is the church.*
>
> EPHESIANS 5:25-31 (NLT)

A man that cannot manage his young children well, whether he is married or parenting alone, can hardly be counted on to manage God's children effectively. Paul said that a minister "*must have a well-behaved family, with children who obey quickly and quietly. For if a man can't make his own little family behave, how can he help the whole church?" 1 Timothy 3:1-5 (TLB)*

The church is the family of God. The church will be no stronger than the individual families that make it up. The families in the congregation take their cues from the ministerial families. Whether it's true or not, most people perceive ministers to be closer to God than the average person. If the gospel that we preach will not work on our families then what hope do the families in the congregation have? Consequently, your family must take first priority in your schedule, in your attention and in your expenditure of energy.

In general, minister's wives are the most neglected, underappreciated, overlooked, criticized, ostracized, scrutinized, and emotionally abused segment of the body. Ministers are sometimes ill-treated also but we often receive public affirmation for our work. Minister's wives receive all of the private acrimony, but little to none of the public applause.

If you are married, you must encourage your wife by making her first priority. No one else will do it. A woman who feels that she must compete with the ministry for her husband's time and attention will eventually become bitter and resentful. It is difficult to compete with something as intangible as "ministry." If all she knows of ministry is that it keeps her husband away from home when she needs him, then "ministry" becomes the enemy. That is why it is so important to help your wife find her niche in ministry. As she partners with you by exercising her gift there will less likely be room for resentment. As you work and pray together, you will grow together. She will be fulfilled in knowing that she is making a significant contribution to the kingdom. If she does not find God's purpose for her life then she can only find pseudo-satisfaction in watching you do what you do. That can only lead to frustration for the both of you because God made you joint-heirs and partners for a reason. Neither of your lives will be complete until both of you are doing what God designed you to do.

Do not try to fit your wife into some type of preformatted minister's wife role. Encourage her to be who God designed her to be, not what other people expect her to be. Every marriage and every individual is different. There is no official or standard way for your wife to interact with your ministry. While every ministerial family should know how to practice the gift of hospitality, not everyone will do it the same way. Some people are outgoing by nature. Others have to work at being comfortable in a crowd. Allow your spouse to grow in Christ according to her temperament and personality.

My wife and I went to a workshop once where the facilitators where a husband and wife team. The husband was a preacher/teacher of some notoriety and had been married to his wife for several decades. We anticipated a great learning experience but were ultimately disappointed for one simple reason. The husband had the gift of teaching, but the wife did not. Because she was married to a great teacher, it was assumed that she could teach as well. She was forced into an arena in which she was not gifted. She was frustrated and so were those who heard her. We all would have been better off if he had done all the teaching and she was allowed to do what she felt comfortable doing.

I experienced the converse situation at another workshop led by a husband and wife team. They were an impressive looking couple from a well-known ministry. He did most of the talking and she supported him. The only problem was she was an excellent teacher but he did not have the gift. Again, the class would have been better if she had done all the teaching and he had prayerfully supported her.

Don't be an Infidel

Ministering to your spouse (or family as the case may be) involves, among other things, providing financial security. Whether you are married or single, the call to the preaching ministry does not necessarily mean it is time to resign from your secular job. It is hard to prepare a sermon when your electricity is cut off. It is not your churches' responsibility to feed and clothe you or your family just because you started preaching. It is the churches' responsibility to feed and clothe your pastor's family because it is foolish to have someone watching over your soul part-time. A pastor needs to give his undivided attention to shepherding the flock. He should not have to divide his time between pastoring and answering to a human boss. If you are not pastoring, however, you need to be working to support your family.

> *If anyone does not provide for his relatives, and especially for his immediate family, he has denied the faith and is worse than an unbeliever.*
>
> 1 TIMOTHY 5:8 (NIV)

You must prayerfully consider how to manage the interplay between your job and your growth in ministry. God may have you at your particular job for a specific reason. There are often tremendous ministry opportunities at the work place for the industrious minister. Lunchtime bible studies, prayer groups and one-on-one witnessing are among the many ways you can impact your work environment. If, however, your job is keeping you from fellowshipping with your home church, because either you always have to work on Sundays, or you stay on the road for significant spans of time, you should aggressively seek other employment. Do not quit your present job until you find a more suitable one but do not become complacent outside of the fellowship.

Some young ministers will never develop like they could because they have never held a full-time job outside of the preaching ministry. Punching in on the clock every day teaches you something about time management. Learning to work with different types of personalities hones your people skills. Navigating office politics and pressures helps you to relate to what parishioners are going through. If all you know is church and church people then in the long run your ministry will not be well rounded and your work ethic is likely to be underdeveloped.

Ministry is what you make it. It is not just what happens on Sunday morning. Ministry is how you make time to pray with a distressed coworker while you are standing at the water cooler. It is foregoing that speaking engagement so you can attend a PTA meeting. It is planning vacations with your family. It is coming home early occasionally, so that your wife can have some time to herself away from the kids.

My Testimony

It took me several years to write this book because I have had to fight to maintain a balance between home, work and public ministry. When God first impressed upon me the need to write something for associate ministers, I was working as an attorney half days and at the church as assistant pastor. Both positions were full-time in terms of energy expended if not in salary. As an attorney, I was able to minister in unique ways by offering free legal services and a Christian presence in venues that are often devoid of a Christian voice.

Over the years, it became increasingly obvious that I would not be able to reach my full potential as an attorney or a minister if I kept doing both. At the same time, I wanted to be a better husband and father. I knew from personal observation and biblical enlightenment that a minister who neglects his family ultimately commits ministerial suicide. I was working 60 hours a week. I wanted to spend more time with my family and we were trying to have another child at the same time. I sought the Lord's guidance and He told me in 1995 to prepare to resign from the law office. He told me that He would make up the loss in income and I believed Him. Nevertheless, I did not resign from the law office until the summer of 1998 because I wanted to be on one accord with my wife. It is easy for me to say, "the Lord told me" this or that but my wife is part of the Body of Christ too and He confirms things through His Body. To leave the law office would mean almost half of our income would vanish.

I have no doubt that she would have stayed by my side if I had resigned earlier, but she would have been doing so out of an legalistic obligation to submit rather than a conviction that God had spoken. By 1998, God blessed us with another child, my wife's faith had increased and she had heard God's voice too. By the time the first edition of this book was printed, I had been out of the law office and in full-time ministry for exactly a year. God is faithful. Since that time missed no meals, we have paid our bills and we have less debt than ever before. I am currently pastoring the best church in the world and living by faith. I present my testimony not as a pattern to follow, but as an example of how God can provide if you keep him first and family a close second.

Chapter 14

When Your Girlfriend Gets Married

What do you do when the church you were campaigning for calls another pastor?

The Holy Spirit is the one who assigns pastors to their posts. (Acts 20:28) The calling of a pastor to a particular venue is a process that is superintended by God himself. Remember that God knows exactly where each member of His body should fit so as to give Him the maximum glory and the church the maximum benefit. If you do not get the church you applied for do not calculate the value of your entire ministry on the outcome of that one event. Do not view it as rejection but rather as protection. God closes doors for many reasons. In general, however, He does it to protect us from the bad and the good until He can provide the best for us.

If someone else got the church you wanted you should make the following adjustments in order to maintain good mental health.

FACE REALITY

I once preached in another city for a pastor's anniversary. When I concluded the sermon I extended an invitation to Christian discipleship. A lady name Sis. Jones came forward during the invitation expressing a desire to make a statement. I could tell the associate in charge was apprehensive about giving her the microphone and that the pastor was likewise wary. When she opened her mouth I understood why. She told the congregation that she had been praying and she wanted the church to pray with her because the Lord had shown her that Bob Smith was to be her husband. Apparently, Bob was not cooperating with her. Bob was in the sanctuary that day but he happened to be sleeping. Unfortunately, Mrs. Bob Smith was there also and wide-awake. Mr. and Mrs. Smith were happily married and had been so for years. Sis. Jones actually did need prayer to help her deal with reality.

In 2001 the Lord placed me at what I consider the best church in the world. During the three years preceding my arrival the church had been through some turmoil and had looked at several candidates. No less than 3 of those candidates came to me personally during my first 6 months as pastor. Each one of them requested prayer because each one had spent years dreaming about pastoring the church I now pastor. Each one of them was having trouble dealing with the reality that what they thought was a sure thing did not turn out the way they expected.

Part of the reason reality was so hard to swallow in both of the cases I mentioned above is that Sis. Jones as those preachers had built elaborate fantasies in their minds. They even felt that God had sanctioned their fantasies. If you are candidating for a church do not allow your heart and mind to create a fantasy situation out what is merely a possibility. Let God move in your behalf. If you do not get the church then pray for the one who did and move on. Do not keep calling the contacts you have in the congregation. Do not sneak by to see what is going on. In the physical realm we call that stalking. In the spiritual realm we call that refusing to deal with reality.

Realize You Are Probably Not "Done" Yet

If you did not get the church you wanted there is a good chance that God is protecting you. Consider the likelihood that either you are not done with your present assignment or your present assignment is not done with you. Perhaps there is a task or two, some goal or objective in God's perfect plan, that you are supposed to accomplish before you leave your current situation. Alternatively, there might be a lesson or two you need to learn at your present assignment before God releases you. Before you graduate you must past your final exams. Every promotion carries with it some sort of promotion test. Perhaps you have not passed your test yet. You might feel like you are ready but God knows if that is the case. There is too much at risk to let you leave the nest unable to fly.

Do What You Can, Where You Are, Without Being Disruptive

When I was a child we used to play kickball all the time. Before the game would start, two captains would choose the players they wanted on their respective teams. Invariably, if the kid who owned the kickball was not chosen by what he or she felt was likely to be the winning team then he or she would say "no fair! I quit!" and take their little red ball and go home.

If you did not get the church you fantasized about do not take your little red ball and go home to pout. You have an affirmative responsibility to do your best with the ministry that is your current reality. Some professional ball players stop putting forth the maximum effort when they do not get traded to the team of their choice. What they do not realize is that they lower their own value in the market by sulking and not playing hard. Do not risk a bad scouting report from heaven. Do what you can where you are until God releases you.

Don't Miss Your Exit

> *"There is an appointed time for everything. And there is a time for every event under heaven — He has made everything appropriate in its time."*
>
> Ecclesiastes 3:1,11

Statistically speaking, the chances are slim that you will stay in one church the duration of your ministry. Most ministry assignments have a shelf life. Make sure you check the expiration date on your current situation. Don't miss your exit.

Some staffing assignments are seasonal while the personal relationships might be permanent. Never confuse your assignment with your relationship. It is possible to move to another assignment while at the same time maintaining a healthy relationship with the spiritual leader you are leaving behind. The nature of human relationships necessitates that they evolve over time.

Generally speaking, sons will eventually leave their father's house in order to start their own families. This does not necessarily mean, however, that something is wrong with you if you have had an extended tenure with your present pastor or if you feel your calling does not include being a senior pastor. Every preacher is not called to pastor. Some are called to assist, accompany and accentuate the ministry of the senior pastor. Others are called to specific areas of ministry such as administration, evangelism, discipleship, or music and worship. Becoming a senior pastor is not the ultimate goal. Doing the will of God is.

Your value to the Body of Christ is not determined by your position or your title. God is looking for and will ultimately reward your faithfulness and fruitfulness regardless of man's estimation of your status. Jesus said,

> *"And whoever in the name of a disciple gives to one of these little ones even a cup of cold water to drink, truly I say to you he shall not lose his reward."*
>
> MATT. 10:42 (NAU)

The Hebrews' writer wrote,

> *"For God is not unjust so as to forget your work and the love which you have shown toward His name, in having ministered and in still ministering to the saints."*
>
> HEB. 6:10 (NAU)

How Will I Know it's Time to Leave?

The Illinois Department of Transportation has provided a practical way to make sure that travelers on Illinois highways do not miss their exits. Several miles before a designated exit the IDOT people will place a sign indicating how many miles ahead the exit is. The objective is to warn the people who are heading to a certain location to start preparing for their exit. Preparation will often include applying the vehicle's turn signal and switching lanes. The traffic in the exit lane must move slower because it is dangerous to attempt to navigate the transition from highway to exit at full speed. In any case, I have never seen a highway exit prepared that the IDOT people did not prepare me for. God is much more considerate and concerned about you than the transportation authorities. If you keep your eyes on the road, He will provide the appropriate signs that it is time to make your exit.

> *"If you go the wrong way-to the right or to the left- you will hear a voice behind you saying, "This is the right way. You should go this way."*
>
> Isaiah 30:21 (NCV)

Common exit signs

You are commissioned

Rev. Thick was the unanimous choice of the pulpit search committee. The chairman of the pulpit search committee tells Rev. Thick, "We love your teaching and preaching. Your vision for the church matches ours perfectly. The vote was 100% in your favor. Oh, and by the way, we will give you a $50,000.00 signing bonus once you agree to become our pastor." Rev. Thick tells the chairman, "Give me a few days to pray about it." A few days later the chairman calls the Thick home and a child answers the phone. "May I speak to Rev. Thick?" he asks. "No, not now," the child replies. "Daddy is upstairs praying." The chairman asks, "Well, may I speak to Mrs. Thick then?" "No, not now," the child replies. "Mama's downstairs packing!"

Do not pray when you should be packing! If God has commissioned you to fill a position then do not snatch defeat from the jaws of victory by waiting around wondering what to do. Do not be afraid to be blessed. If you prayed specifically and God answered specifically then call the movers and start packing! *The blessing of the LORD brings wealth, and he adds no trouble to it. Proverbs 10:22 (NIV)*

You are dismissed

Not every story ends with "and they lived happily ever after." Not every employment situation ends with a retirement celebration and a gold watch. Not every ministry assignment ends on good terms. If you were asked to find another place to worship by your pastor then do not try to play Samson and bring down the whole house with you. Face reality and move on.

Sometimes God has to force us to move in order to bless us. Though the process might be painful never doubt the fact that God is causing all things to work together for good. (Romans 8:28) It could be that you missed some other exit signs and God decided that in order to rescue you He had to force you out of your comfort zone. An eaglet would never leave the comfort of the nest if the mother eagle did not make it so uncomfortable that the eaglet was forced out. Do not fight dismissal; it may be God's way of promoting you. Before you leave, however, check yourself based upon the principles contained in the section entitled "Leaving Well."

While in Sodom you start smelling smoke.

I would like to think that every building that has the words "church" or "worship center" on its marquee is filled with consecrated, Spirit-filled, Bible-practicing Christians. I would also like to think that every pastor is sold out to the Lord. Unfortunately, we live in fallen world filled with fallen people who are just as prone to sin as we are. More tragic is the fact that, through the lack of accountability, some religious leaders can develop sinful patterns of behavior that infect the very culture of the church. Such was the case in Corinth. The church culture has been so desensitized that a man in the membership was openly sleeping with his step-mother and the church said nothing about it. (1 Corinthians 5:1-2) People were getting drunk at the Communion service. (1 Corinthians 11:21) They were being disorderly in the worship service. (1 Corinthians 14) Unfortunately, there are some contemporary churches where the strongholds of adultery, alcoholism, drug abuse, homosexuality, lesbianism and rebellion have become part of the culture.

When wrong is sanctioned as right and you look wrong for doing right, then it is time for you to look for the nearest exit. God loves His church more than any one of us can fathom and He can change any situation. But the fact that

He can change the culture does not mean that he will use you to do it. When sin in the church becomes pandemic then deliverance invariably requires mass repentance that starts with the leadership. If the leadership in your church is unwilling to confront egregious sin to the point that rebellion, substance abuse and sexual sin is practiced openly without censure the next stop is "Judgment" and you might want to look for the exit before you get there.

Your brook dries up

Sometimes God moves us not because there is something wrong with our present situation or us as individuals. Sometimes He moves us because we have become too comfortable where we are and someone else needs our help. When your effectiveness and the favor of God on your ministry in your present location start to dry up it might mean that there is another assignment waiting for you.

The life of Elijah illustrates this point. When God commissioned a drought in the land He sustained Elijah at the brook Cherith. Once the brook dried up it was time for Elijah to move to Zarephath because there was a single parent there who needed his help. (I Kings 17:5-15) If Elijah had stayed at the brook the widow and her family would likely have starved to death.

Sometimes your brook just dries up. The anointing does not flow with ease in areas where the Spirit once gave you great effectiveness. There is nothing wrong with you or your relationship with your pastor or the membership. It is just time to move on. God uses dried up brooks and missing ravens to get us to move to the next assignment.

LEAVING WELL

When it is time for you to leave your present assignment, make sure you leave right. You never know when you might need to come back.

Don't Muddy the Water

> *"Is it not enough for you to feed on the good pasture? Must you also trample the rest of your pasture with your feet? Is it not enough for you to drink clear water? Must you also muddy the rest with your feet? Must my flock feed on what you have trampled and drink what you have muddied with your feet?"*
>
> EZEKIEL 34:18-19 (NIV)

You were blessed to have been in the assignment you are now in the process of leaving. You learned some invaluable lessons while your were there whether you learned what to do or what not to do. While you might be moving on there are those who will remain in that place. Do not dishonor God and disrespect the house by taking all the clear benefits and then leaving muddy water behind you. You muddy the water when you divulge secrets, indiscretions and weaknesses that you learned by being up close to the pastor. You muddy the water when you criticize and condemn the practices and approach of the current leadership on your way out the door. You muddy the water when you remain silent while others vocalize personal bitterness toward the leadership. Your silence amounts to tacit agreement. Leave the house with clean feet so that when you get to your new home you will not be tracking in any mud. You cannot start clean if you leave messy.

Don't Rustle the Sheep

> *And from among your own selves men will arise, speaking perverse things, to draw away the disciples after them.*
>
> ACTS 20:30 (NAU)

If you engage in ministry for any appreciable amount of time in a particular setting you are going to develop a following whether you want to or not. If you are relocating to a place that is in driving distance from your last assignment then resist the temptation to steal the sheep that you once tended. They will naturally want to follow you if they were blessed by your ministry. God is not moving you so that you can transplant the church you are leaving. He is moving you so that He can multiply not subtract.

There is no shortage of sinners where you are going. If you teach, preach, evangelize and disciple people, you will have more than enough new converts to concern yourself with. There is no need to rob your pastor's aquarium when there is a lake full of fish right at your doorstep. Use your influence to encourage the friends you leave behind to keep progressing right where they are. They already have a shepherd; you go after the lost sheep.

Don't Burn Your Bridges (or Your Britches)

Some associates leave places owing money to the church and apologies to the membership. Do not make the mistake of trying to take advantage of the membership because you think you will not see most of them again. You do not know who is related to whom. The young lady whose affections you toy with before you leave might be the distant cousin of your new chairman of trustees. The brother from whom you borrow that large sum of money might be the high school classmate of your new choir director. Keep your relationships intact because you never know when you might need to come home. The bridge that brought you over might need to bring you back.

Keep your britches (pants) intact also. By britches or pants I am referring to the fact that you should not let yourself get into compromising situations that would cause you to lose your pants. Though Joseph did nothing wrong he was charged and found guilty or aggravated sexual assault because he could not provide a satisfactory explanation for why Mrs. Potiphar had his pants. Do not let the euphoria of leaving coax you into thinking that you can let your guard down as it relates to integrity and purity. Many one night stands turn into courtroom dramas because two people thought they were never going to see each other again and let their passions run amok. Leave with your pants in hand and your reputation above reproach.

Don't Sow What You Aren't Willing to Reap

Do not be deceived, God is not mocked; for whatever a man sows, this he will also reap.

GALATIANS 6:7 (NAU)

The biblical prescription is church planting not church splitting. Though there are church splits that ultimately survive and even thrive, I believe they are the exception and not the rule. God cannot bless rebellion against His established order and remain true to His word and His character. Psalms 147:17 (NCV) says, *"Everything the LORD does is right. He is loyal to all he has made."*

If you are contemplating organizing a church out of the church you currently serve in without your pastor's blessing you are treading on dangerous ground. If you are determined to do it then you should remember the law of the harvest. You will not only reap what you sow but you will reap more of it. You might sow the wind but you will reap the whirlwind. (Hosea 8:7) Would you want one of your associates to treat you like you are currently treating your pastor? If you are sure that you are called to pastor, why can't you accept a vacant church that is already established somewhere else? If you feel called to organize a church, why do you have to take established members from your present church when there are so many people in your community who have never heard the Gospel? What is your real motive and what Biblical model can you point to that justifies your approach? Pastoring is hard enough when God ordains and orchestrates your placement. If you plot, plan and place yourself, then do not be surprised if someone plots and plans to replace you.

Don't Leave Your Room a Mess

> *I have fought the good fight, I have finished the race, I have kept the faith.*
>
> 2 TIMOTHY 4:7

Make sure that you complete your assignments before you leave. If that is impossible to do at least provide some sort of written report on your progress. Do not leave your area of responsibility in such disarray that the next person has to start from scratch because they cannot decipher what was going on.

While I was in seminary I served as Youth Director and Minister of Music at a church on the west coast. Nine months before graduation I realized that I would probably be moving back to the Midwest once I matriculated. With my pastor's supervision and guidance I trained my replacements and put together a working manual that described the how, what, why, where, when and who of each ministry I was involved in. Consequently, the ministries were able to move forward without rebuilding from square one.

If you end your old assignment on a good note you can start your new assignment with a clear conscience. Leave in such a way that you can always come back if you need to.

Action Points *Make the Peace*

"If it is possible, as far as it depends on you, live at peace with everyone." Rom. 12:18

- ❑ Have you ever been a candidate for senior pastor? How did you feel about the process?
- ❑ How long have you been at your present assignment? How long do you anticipate staying there?
- ❑ Have you ever thought about pastoring? Do you think you are prepared to pastor right now? Why or why not?
- ❑ If you are married, ask your wife if she thinks you are ready to pastor. If you have children ask them if they believe you would make a good pastor.
- ❑ What would it take for you to leave your present church home?

Chapter 15

PASTOR DADDY

People as diverse as Malcolm X, Dr. Martin Luther King, Jr., Aretha Franklin and Denzel Washington have all had to work through the same issue; growing up as a preacher's kid. Preacher's children have been stereotyped as being some of the worst children in the congregation. Whether that stereotype is accurate or not, the undeniable truth is that your relationship with your father has a tremendous impact on how you handle life. Some rebel, some excel. When your father is your pastor, then you have a unique set of challenges to face. If you are serving with your father as an associate or an assistant then the following guidelines will help you safely navigate the delicate tension between you, your father and the congregation.

SAGE ADVICE

"Never let people, or anything else, separate you from your father." That is what a seasoned pastor told me the day after I publicly acknowledged my call to the preaching ministry. Since that time I have witnessed why his warning was so timely. People and circumstances have a way of driving a wedge between you and your father if you let them. Some congregants will openly try to compare you with your father and foster in you a false sense of superiority. Others will compare you unfavorably with your father and try to foster a sense of competition. Still others might be bold enough to complain to you about your father's decisions or policies. Whatever the case do not allow people to disrupt the relationship between you and your father.

Similarly, do not allow circumstances or a lack of communication drive you and your father apart. There will be times that you will disagree with him. Whether it is a practical concern or a doctrinal issue, there is a way to disagree on a matter without being disagreeable. Always treat your father with respect whether in private or public. If you have had the benefit of a formal education and you father has not, you still must acknowledge and appreciate his position and perspective. Ultimately God is only going to hold you responsible for what you can control. Since you are not the pastor, then do not get bent out of shape if your father/pastor makes a decision that you disagree with.

Do not take it personally

Some pastors are able to take advice from their children. Others disregard what their children have to say. More than likely your father is living within the tension of trusting your loyalty and doubting your competence. The reason you get to work up close with him is his confidence in your loyalty. He raised you and knows that you have his best interest at heart. The familiarity that comes along with having raised you, however, is what makes doubting your competence such a subtle temptation. It is not that your father thinks that you are incompetent. It is just difficult to fathom that God has placed the answer to a complex ministry problem in the mind of the one who seemingly a short while ago was worried about proms and pimples. Obviously pride can play a part in the relationship dynamics also. Some fathers feel obligated to have all of the answers all of the time. Whatever the case may be, do not take it personally if all of your suggestions are not acted upon.

FOCUS ON WHAT YOU CAN DO, NOT ON WHAT YOU CANNOT DO

You might see the need to start a new ministry or to revamp an old one. Maybe there is a new curriculum that just came out that you believe would benefit the ministry. Perhaps you have talents, skills, abilities or training that you believe are being underused. You will waste a lot of emotional energy if you focus all of you attention on what you are prohibited from doing. Do what you can and do it well. God might be trying to direct you to a more fruitful level of maturity and impact by restricting you. Consider Paul's experience in Acts 16:16:6-7 (TEV)

> *They travelled through the region of Phrygia and Galatia because the Holy Spirit did not let them preach the message in the province of Asia. When they reached the border of Mysia, they tried to go into the province of Bithynia, but the Spirit of Jesus did not allow them.*

If you read the rest of the story you will find that Paul was directed by the Spirit to go to Macedonia and preach there. What seemed to be a restriction ultimately turned out to be God's guidance mechanism. Paul might not have considered Macedonia unless Asia and Bithynia were prohibited.

Write down what you see and how you would do things differently. Some of the ideas that you have would not work in your father's ministry because the timing is wrong or the needed resources are not in place. God might be showing you some areas of the ministry that need improvement not so that you can do something about it but so you can pray about it. Maybe you are not the savior of your father's ministry but a servant of the Kingdom. If the King has given you a good idea then he will also give you the right platform and the right season to implement that idea.

LET YOUR WORK ETHIC AND INTEGRITY SILENCE YOUR CRITICS

Some people at your church do not like your father. Some of those same people will not like you because you are your father's child. Some will charge your father with nepotism if you are on staff at the church. Others will discount your ministry by reminding you, and everyone else, that they helped raise you and what an obnoxious child you used to be. You will never overcome unwarranted negativity by verbally attacking your detractors. Let your work speak for you.

> *Do not let anyone look down on you because you are young, but be an example for the believers in your speech, your conduct, your love, faith, and purity.*
>
> I TIMOTHY 4:12 (TEV)

If you handle your business then even your detractors will have respect for you. You must be willing to pay the price, however, to discipline your time and energy and to keep your behavior above reproach. Ultimately no one can argue with excellence and integrity. Even if they try God will work in your favor. (1 Peter 3:16)

Develop a Realistic Attitude

Most people do not know how to treat their pastor. We usually go to one of two extremes. Either we treat him like a god or like a dog. Neither extreme is biblical. When you complicate matters by serving under your father as an associate, then the balance needed is even more delicate. You must learn how to honor him without deifying him while at the same time accepting his faults without demoralizing him.

Do not take your father's greatness for granted. Having grown up in your father's home you know something about his dirty laundry. You are aware of his faults, failures and foibles. Armed with such knowledge, it is easy to forget that your father is a God-appointed pastor to a mass of people. He might just be "Dad" to you but he is someone else's spiritual leader. If he has pastored any significant number of years then he has impacted hundreds if not thousands of lives. What you have memorized from his repertoire of favorite sayings and now consider stale is like fresh manna to most of the people who hear him. He has been appointed by God to watch over souls. You owe him the utmost esteem if for nothing else for his work's sake.

Head of Gold, Feet of Clay

Your father has limitations, flaws and blind spots just like every other human being. A necessary part of growing into full maturity is learning how to handle our father's humanity. When the Bible says "all have sinned" it includes your father too. As great a preacher, teacher and pastor as your father may be you must recognize that he is as human as all of the rest of us. Consequently, he has to struggle with the same temptations and character flaws that we all do. Be realistic about his sins and shortcomings. He might be blind to some of his weaknesses. Other sinful habits or patterns of behavior may be more blatant. The bottom line is that you do not have to follow the negative examples that he sets. If there is a history of abuse, promiscuity or addiction in you family, the cycle can end with you. Be honest about what you have seen and what you have experienced and then let God deliver you. It will not be easy neither will it be instantaneous. Nevertheless, your teeth do not have to be set on edge because of the sour grapes your father ate.

Deal with your father's humanity like you would a good piece of fried fish. Eat the meat but leave the bone. Pick out the good parts and leave the rest alone.

Action Points *All in the family*

- ❑ In your opinion, what are the advantages of having your father as pastor? What are the disadvantages?
- ❑ If there was one thing you could change about your relationship with your father, what would it be?
- ❑ What is your fondest memory of growing up in a pastor's home? What is your worst memory?
- ❑ How would you complete the following sentence: Most people would respect my father more if they knew ____________________________.

-Epilogue-

BEFORE YOU SAY I DO

You would not marry a woman without knowing something about her background, would you? Regardless of how good she looked on the outside you would want to know some pertinent information before you asked her to marry you; such as:

- Do you have a criminal background?
- Is there a history of mental illness in your family?
- What happened in your last relationship?
- How many times have you been married before?
- If we get married, who is going to handle the money?

This list is not exhaustive but illustrative of the type of information you need before you make a lifelong commitment to someone. Once you have the information, you can make an informed choice. Just because she is crazy does not mean you should not marry her. Just make sure she takes her medication.

Pastoring a church is like being married. One day someone might propose to you. Before you accept the proposal make sure you ask some questions. Here is a sample list of questions to get you started.

Past Relationships

What happened to the last pastor?

If he is alive, where is he now?

If he died, how did he die?

How many pastors has this church had?

How long did each of them stay?

What kind of leader was the most recent pastor?

Since the last pastor left, who has been running things?

Church Bylaws (Ask for a copy)

Is the church incorporated as a nonprofit organization?

Is the pastor an employee or chairman of the board of directors?

Is the board of directors comprised of the trustees, the deacon board or both?

How are trustees selected?

What is the procedure for removing the pastor?

How can the bylaws be amended?

Who has the final word on hiring and firing decisions?

Who controls the money?

Church History and Demographics

How did the church get to this location?

Have there been any church splits?

What kind of debt does the church currently have?

How many members are on roll?

How many members are active?

How many attend Sunday School?

How many attend Prayer Meeting?

What is the average age of the membership?

How many people were baptized last year?

How many came by Christian experience?

Compensation Package

How is the pastor's salary determined?

Does the salary include a housing allowance?

Will the church pay for insurance benefits?

Does the package include a ministry related reimbursement account?

What type of insurance coverage will be offered? Medical? Dental? Optical? Disability?

How many weeks vacation per year?

Does the pastor receive regular love offerings?

Does the pastor have an anniversary?

Who pays for pastor's attendance at conventions, convocations and conferences?

Who will pay for moving expenses?

Vision

Where does the current leadership see the church heading in the next 5 to 10 years?

What is this churches unique contribution to this community?

Why is this church in this neighborhood?

What kind of pastor are you looking for?

What do you expect the pastor to do that is not being done now?

Doctrinal Essentials

What is the churches stance on the inerrancy of scripture?

What is the churches stance on the eternal security of the believer?

What is the churches stance on divorce and remarriage?

What is the churches stance on homosexuality?

What is the churches stance on pastoral authority?

What is the churches stance on women in the preaching ministry?

Ministers

How many associate ministers are there?

What are their roles?

Is there an assistant pastor?

How many associates are ordained?

Church Polity and Staff

Does the church have an official board?

Who makes the final decision on matters of concerning doctrine?

Who makes the financial decisions?

Are the deacons and trustees separate or are the deacons the trustees?

Who has the final say in staffing decisions (i.e., hiring and firing)?

How many full-time staff members does the church have? How long have they been employed at the church?

Who evaluates the staff?

Parting Words of Wisdom

The Holy Spirit appoints pastors to churches. (Acts 20:28) Do not try to manipulate your way into a situation. Whoever places you has the power to keep you or remove you.

Talk to older pastors in the community. Find out what kind of reputation the church has before you accept it. If the previous pastor is still alive, contact him and listen to what he has to say. A little research up front can save a lot of heartache down the road. Be prayerful and seek godly counsel. Sometimes the excitement of being considered for a church can blind you to the red flags God keeps raising.

Wait your turn. God knows where you are. He sees what you are going through. Do not "marry" the first church that proposes to you just so you can get away from "home." Wait on the Lord and seek His face.

> *For I know the plans I have for you," declares the LORD, "plans to prosper you and not to harm you, plans to give you hope and a future. Then you will call upon me and come and pray to me, and I will listen to you. You will seek me and find me when you seek me with all your heart.*
>
> JEREMIAH 29:11-13 (NIV)